Writing Short Stories and Articles

If you want to know how . . .

Creative Writing
*Use your imagination, develop your writing skills
and get published*

Writing a Children's Book
How to write for children and get published

Write & Sell Your Novel
The beginner's guide to writing for publication

Awaken the Writer Within
Release your creativity and find your true writer's voice

The Writer's Guide to Getting Published

howtobooks

Please send for a free copy of the latest catalogue:

How To Books
3 Newtec Place, Magdalen Road,
Oxford OX4 1RE, United Kingdom
email: info@howtobooks.co.uk
http://www.howtobooks.co.uk

Writing Short Stories and Articles

How to get your work published in newspapers and magazines

3rd edition

ADÈLE RAMET

howtobooks

First published by How To Books Ltd,
3 Newtec Place, Magdalen Road,
Oxford OX4 1RE. United Kingdom.
Tel: (01865) 793806. Fax: (01865) 248780.
email: info@howtobooks.co.uk
www.howtobooks.co.uk

First published 1998
Reprinted 1998, 1999
Second edition 2001
Third edition 2004

British Library Cataloguing in Publication Data
A catalogue record for this book is available from the British Library

Cartoons by Simon Ramet
Cover design by Baseline Arts Ltd, Oxford
Produced for How To Books by Deer Park Productions, Tavistock
Typeset by PDQ Typesetting, Newcastle-under-Lyme, Staffordshire
Printed and bound by Cromwell Press, Trowbridge

Note: The material contained in this book is set out in good faith for
general guidance and no liability can be accepted
for loss or expense incurred as a result of relying in particular
circumstances on statements made in the book. The laws and
regulations are complex and liable to change, and readers should
check the current position with the relevant authorities before making
personal arrangements.

Contents

List of Illustrations

Preface

ARTICLE OR SHORT STORY?

Newspapers and magazines are two of the most attainable markets for article and short story writers keen to see their work in print.

Many a struggling writer's first taste of success may well have been the letters page of their local newspaper or favourite magazine. Moved to put pen to paper by a local injustice, an amusing incident or just because they enjoy writing letters, the pleasure of being published is invariably addictive.

Once hooked on publication, the true writer will be unable to stop and the letters will begin their inevitable metamorphosis into an article or story. It is at this stage that we need to pause and consider the options open to the freelance contributor.

Bearing in mind that the majority of topical hard news stories are provided by professional journalists and staff writers, this still leaves plenty of scope for the freelance in the form of feature articles and short stories. It is, therefore, extremely useful to develop the ability to write both fact and fiction.

For those writers familiar with journalistic references to news *stories*, the distinction between an article and a story may be unclear. Is it fact or fiction? Indeed, when is a story not a story? At first sight, some of the definitions for the word 'story' given in *Chambers Dictionary* simply add to the confusion:

- a fictitious narrative
- a tale
- an anecdote
- a news article.

However, as every successful freelance knows, the answer to the riddle, 'When is a story not a story?' is probably 'When it's an article'. Whilst the format may differ, the approach by the writer is surprisingly similar.

This book is designed to give writers an insight into both the similarities and the differences between producing fictional short stories and non-fiction articles for the magazine and newspaper markets. The key to both formats is:

- brevity
- clarity
- reader identification.

One discipline relies heavily on the ability to place factual information in a logical order in a manner that is easily absorbed by the reader. The other requires the writer to have a sound grasp of fiction writing techniques. As you work your way through this book, you will discover that these elements are to be found in varying proportions in both genres.

This book takes you step by step through the techniques of writing both articles and short stories. It shows you how to write to length and style, how to adapt your work for different markets and how the inclusion of fiction techniques can enhance and improve factual articles. Research and the importance of factual accuracy in fiction will be explained and guidance is given on how to present and market your finished manuscripts.

Master the requirements of both genres and you will double your chances of writing successfully for newspapers and magazines.

Adèle Ramet

Acknowledgements

I would like to thank freelance writers Jill Eckersley, Kate Nivison and Gillian Thornton for their supportive and encouraging words of advice.

My thanks also to twist authors Joyce Begg, Fred Clayson and E. Evans, Groundwork Bridgend, Linda Sutton and the following editors for their patience and generous co-operation in the writing of this book:

Linda O'Byrne and Clare Swatman of *Bella*
Pat Richardson of *Best*
Janina Pogorzelski of *The Lady*
Jacqueline Branch of *Chat*
Helen Christie of *Mslexia*
Liz Smith of *My Weekly*
Gaynor Davies of *Woman's Weekly*
Bridget Davidson of *Yours*

A very special thank you is due to my family for all their practical support in the writing of this book and for always being there for me when I need them.

Adèle Ramet

1

Mixing Fact and Fiction

The motivation to write for publication differs widely from one writer to another. Many start at school, writing essays and stories in their English lessons. Consistently high marks from a teacher they respect in a subject they enjoy may well plant the seed of hope that one day, in the far distant future, they may try their hand at writing a novel.

For others, it is the school magazine that shapes their ambition. A series of articles, possibly leading to their taking over the editor's chair and before you know it, a future non-fiction feature writer is born.

Picking up the threads

Whilst these early enthusiasms can lead to a career as a professional journalist, the vast majority of us simply place these ambitions in the same unattainable category as rock star or racing driver and go about our more mundane daily lives.

However, for many of us there comes a time, prompted perhaps by redundancy, children leaving home or simply the belief that we can do better than the author of the article or short story we've just read, when our thoughts return to those early writing successes of our schooldays.

Our choice of fact or fiction is invariably influenced by our past interests and, eager to pick up the threads where we left off, we feel we have to return to either one or the other. However, just because you were good at articles in the past, doesn't mean you can't write short stories now, and vice versa.

Understanding the differences

Before we begin to explore the many similarities, it is useful to establish exactly what differences there are between the two genres. The chart in Figure 1 highlights the main points which separate factual articles from fictional short stories.

Articles	Stories
Fact, i.e. the truth	Fiction, i.e. a lie
Primarily informative	Primarily entertaining
Author can provide own illustrations	Illustrations always provided by magazine
Quotations from other published articles add credibility	Quotations from published authors can spoil the fictional flow
The ending can be either downbeat or uplifting depending upon the theme and purpose of the article	Most magazine short stories require an upbeat ending

Fig. 1. The differences between factual articles and fictional stories.

ESTABLISHING COMMON GROUND

Perhaps the best way to distinguish between the two

genres is to remember that fiction writers tell lies whilst article writers tell the truth. Well, most of the time anyway.

Having established the main differences, we now need to look at the common ground. This comes from the techniques the writer needs to employ in order to communicate effectively with the reader.

Short stories and articles both require:

- a beginning, a middle and an ending which ties up satisfactorily with the beginning
- a strong, attention-grabbing opening which gives an indication of what is to follow
- accurate factual information
- clear imagery
- reader identification
- content which reflects the style of the newspaper or magazine for which it is intended.

Both genres must also:

- be written to a predetermined length
- have an original slant
- hold the reader's attention from beginning to end
- deliver what was promised in the opening line.

One extra ingredient which is optional for the article but is usually considered essential for a short story is:

- a proportion of dialogue.

All these points will be explained as you work through the book, but as you can already see, there are many factors which are common to both genres.

EXPLOITING THE SIMILARITIES

Having gained an insight into the techniques required to write fact and fiction, we can exploit the similarities to enable us to write productively for newspapers and magazines.

Beginning with an idea

Imagine the scene. In the hope of selling an article to your local newspaper, you are attending a school fête. A wide variety of animals have been entered for the annual pet show, but your attention is drawn to the dogs' obedience competition where, you are told, this year's winner is an ill-treated animal, rescued by the RSPCA.

In addition to a general report on the fête, you now have the opportunity to write a whole range of articles for a selection of outlets, from specialist magazines for dog-owners to mass market publications. There is scope for:

◆ a feature about the dog and its owner
◆ a feature about pet shows in general
◆ a report on the work of the RSPCA
◆ an in-depth investigation into cruelty to animals
◆ a step-by-step guide to dog training
◆ a report highlighting the special problems involved in taking on a rescue pet.

At this stage, you are still only looking at topics associated with dogs but there will have been a range of pets at the show, including some exotic animals which could give rise to all sorts of article ideas.

Finding a story

The possibilities for articles are extensive but so, too, are the possibilities for fiction.

Pets have a knack of bringing people together and offer any number of situations for romantic fiction. Two lonely people walking their dogs in the park, a kind stranger offering to help rescue a cat from a tree or someone returning a lost pet to its rightful owner.

Animals also provide the opportunity for conflict between their owners and where there is conflict, there is potential not only for romance but also for a twist in the tale.

For example, keen gardeners can be highly intolerant of a neighbour's wandering cat. Where a potentially prize-winning plant is under severe threat from the unwanted attentions of a pedigree pussycat, more than a little fur will fly in the days leading up to the local fête.

PLAYING AROUND WITH THE FACTS

Earlier in this chapter, I stated that fiction writers tell lies, whilst article writers tell the truth. The truth is, that this statement was a lie.

Telling lies

Whilst a good article is based firmly in fact, there is nothing wrong with employing one or two fiction-writing tricks of the trade in order to liven up a piece of non-fiction.

You may, for example, be writing a personal experience article about the problems you encountered on your first ever caravan holiday. As the article begins to take shape, you are reminded of an amusing incident which took place on a much later trip.

By this time, you had owned a caravan for several years and were experienced enough to know better but with a little tweaking here and there, the anecdote offers some handy hints on caravan towing and serves to round off the article perfectly.

OK, so maybe you have drastically altered the sequence of events in order to embellish the feature, but politics is not the only profession where being economical with the truth can be highly effective in achieving the desired result.

READING ABOUT PEOPLE

Whether fact or fiction, people read about people. Factual articles which include case histories, informal chats, quotes and photographs are far more interesting than those which simply list a lot of statistical information.

Expanding the 'I' element

As article writers, we are advised to write about what we know and in order to establish credibility, we need to include details of our own personal experience. However, one of the biggest pitfalls for the novice writer is the 'I' element, as demonstrated in Example A below:

Example A

My first caravan holiday was a total disaster. The first thing I did wrong was to forget to make everything secure for travelling. Then I left the milk behind and I hadn't gone more than a few miles along the motorway before I was pulled over by the police.

By now, any experienced caravanner will have lost patience with the writer and inexperienced readers will have gained no concrete information. This is one person's own story and is of no interest to anyone else.

The first thing the writer needs to do is to replace the word 'I' with the word 'you'. This brings in the element which is essential for both fact and fiction, that of reader identification. In other words, the reader must be able to relate to the people and situations featured in your articles and short stories. The rewritten Example B offers this element to the reader:

Example B

If you're planning to tour with a caravan for the first time, you're in for a rare treat. No other holiday combines the same kind of freedom with the luxury a well-equipped caravan provides. That isn't to say that there aren't one or two pitfalls, but by following a few simple rules they can be easily avoided.

In the next chapter, we'll be looking at different types of articles and formats you can use, but the above sample is an illustration of the opening to a straightforward factual information piece.

CHANGING WITH THE SEASONS

One of the biggest headaches facing an editor is finding suitable features and stories which reflect the changing seasons and significant days throughout the annual calendar.

Keeping one step ahead

We will be looking at **topicality** later in the book, but for now, bear in mind that the writer who an editor can call upon to fill a seasonal slot is always in demand. Editors are invariably looking for articles and stories which not only reflect seasonal changes in the weather but also the following events on the annual calendar:

- Christmas
- St Valentine's Day
- Easter
- All Fool's Day
- Mothering Sunday
- Father's Day
- Halloween.

They will also require features commemorating anniversaries of historical events and influential figures, holiday ideas for 'Summer Specials' and educational items for 'Back to School' editions. There will be more information on planning ahead for these issues in Chapter 10.

TAKING A FLEXIBLE APPROACH

For the short story writer, the magazine market is quite specific. Ages and lifestyles of characters will be heavily influenced by the readership of the magazines at which you are aiming and because magazine styles are very distinctive, the market for any one particular storyline may be quite limited.

As the fiction market is so restrictive, rather than waste good research material by confining it to one or perhaps two short stories, it pays to put any facts you have discovered to good use in the form of a number of different articles.

Getting the most out of the material

Never allow anything to go to waste. Your cupboards and drawers will quickly become stuffed with newspaper cuttings, press releases, information leaflets and any other useful material you can lay your hands on, but it will be worth it in the end.

It certainly pays to be flexible. Set out all the facts you have available, the seasonal implications, the people involved, then consider the uses to which you can put all the information. Fact, fiction or a mixture of both, anything's worth a try.

CASE STUDIES

George tells his story

George has led a full and active life and, since his retirement, has taken up a number of hobbies. His anecdotes about his work and the people he meets in pursuit of his interests are fun to listen to but are far too personal to interest anyone who does not know him. He uses the word 'I' constantly and until he stands back from the incidents he relates and puts them in a broader context, he will fail in his bid to achieve publication.

John shares his expertise

John is an office worker in his late thirties. Like George, he has several hobbies about which he is both enthusiastic and knowledgeable. His articles and short stories are always written with a specific readership in mind and are designed to both inform and to entertain. His subject expertise brings an authority to his work which adds an important dimension to everything that he writes.

CHECKLIST

1. Are you sure you know the difference between an article and a short story?

2. Do you have sufficient factual information for an article?

3. Can you turn some of your facts into a short story?

4. Does the word 'you' feature significantly in your article?

5. Will a reader relate to the people and situations you are writing about?

ASSIGNMENT

Think of a single theme based on your own interest and expertise and write down as many different article ideas as you can. When you've finished, go back and see how many of those ideas could be adapted into fictional short stories.

$$\left(2\right)$$

Constructing an Article

HOOKING THE READER

When you sit down to write
an article, there are two main
points to bear in
mind:

1. the topic you are writing about
2. the person who will read it.

Selecting the right topics

There is no doubt that you will
get better results if you write
about what you know rather
than if you attempt to write
authoritatively on a subject
with which you are unfamiliar.

Writing for the reader

The key to writing effective articles is not to write for
yourself but to inform and entertain the reader.

Let's say that your hobby is decorating eggs and you want
to write an article about it. Don't be tempted to set up the
background in a lengthy introduction about yourself or
your reader will have completely lost interest by the time
the topic is revealed.

Grabbing the reader's attention

If you are to grab and hold a reader's attention, it is essential to tell them what the article is about in the very first line. A good opening should:

◆ be short and to the point
◆ tell you the topic in the first line
◆ give you a hint of what is to come.

To illustrate the point, which of the following two openings would make you want to read on?

Opening A

I began my hobby many years ago when my parents took me on holiday to a tiny village in the country. However, it was many years later before I was able to take it up, long after my family had grown up and left home and I was able to devote more time to my own hobbies and interests. It took me ages to gather together the materials I needed, find a place to store them and clear a space in the house for me to work and then a close relative became ill and I had to help look after them, so that put paid to any plans of my own.

Opening B

With a final brush stroke, Sheila's latest work is complete and she adds a highly decorative goose egg to her large collection of handpainted eggs.

Sheila began decorating eggs over thirty years ago. She uses mainly chicken and goose eggs, but before she starts a new design, the first step is to blow and clean her 'canvas'.

In Opening A, the first line fails to reveal the subject of the article and you are none the wiser by the end of the paragraph. No editor would bother reading beyond this point, but should the piece somehow find its way into print, few readers would be persuaded to struggle on.

Opening B, on the other hand, gives you the topic in the first sentence. It introduces a person with whom the reader can identify and you have an indication that the article will be a step-by-step introduction to egg decoration.

An article of this type would be most suitable for either a local interest or a craft/hobby publication. In this case, your reader will be a person who enjoys arts and crafts and will expect concrete information about the topic, not a rambling piece detailing the life and times of someone they have never met.

Learning something new

Providing you choose subjects you find interesting, there is no reason why you shouldn't research and write about topics you know little about. Just bear in mind that an article you find boring to write will be even more boring for a stranger to read. Because people read about people, you can enliven the piece with the inclusion of a little background information about the person practising the craft and some dialogue with them.

DRAFTING AN OUTLINE

Having decided upon a topic, it is worth taking the time to sort out exactly what points you intend to cover.

Writing an outline along the lines of the one shown in Figure 2 will give you a framework for the piece and keep your mind focused on the task in hand. As we shall see later in this chapter, it is all too easy to wander away from the main theme and an outline should prevent this.

KEEPING TO THE POINT

An outline should be treated as a flexible framework on which to base your article. Once devised, the next stage is to consider the content in more detail and this is where your mind has a habit of wandering off the point.

BEGINNING	Introduction to the craft, history, popularity and to Sheila, the artist.
MIDDLE	Sheila's background.
	Egg decorating step by step.
	Explain how reader can get started and lead in to closing paragraphs.
END	Materials, stockists, costs, courses, reference books, useful addresses and contact numbers, etc.
	Tie up with opening.

Fig. 2. Sample outline for an article on egg decorating.

Condensing the content

Having opened the egg decorating article quite economically, we have set the tone for a straight, no-frills, information piece.

Using the outline in Figure 2 as a guide, the middle paragraphs should not only contain a factual guide to egg painting but also some personal information about Sheila and some dialogue with her. This should be as brief as possible but with sufficient detail to satisfy the reader's natural curiosity and establish Sheila's credibility as a skilled practitioner of her craft. Something along the following lines would be suitable:

Sheila has been decorating eggs for over thirty years and still has the first one she ever attempted at the age of 14. On leaving college, she worked as an art teacher for several years before staying at home to bring up her family.

'During this period,' she explained, 'I had time to develop my egg decorating skills and was eventually approached to run classes at my local community centre.'

In addition to teaching, Sheila now offers her highly decorative eggs for sale in a number of specialist outlets throughout the country...

Link the middle and the closing paragraphs with something like, 'Sheila advises anyone interested in taking up the hobby to...', and go on to list the steps the reader should take.

Referring once more to the outline, you can see that the following practical reference information should be given in the concluding paragraphs:

- ◆ materials and costs
- ◆ stockists (including mail order details)
- ◆ addresses (including telephone numbers and email addresses) of courses, websites and costs if available
- ◆ useful books including details of publishers and prices.

Rounding off the piece

Finally, the article should be brought to a close by rounding it off with a reference to the opening. For example, the following paragraph closes the piece by mirroring the opening references to Sheila and the topic itself:

> For Sheila, knowing that people are prepared to buy her work is an added bonus. The true satisfaction is seeing a humble hen's egg transformed into a decorative work of art.

LAYING IT OUT LOGICALLY

With the sort of subject matter featured in the egg decorating example, putting the information in a logical order is relatively simple.

Piecing it all together

Having settled on a topic and a suitable readership, the format for the article was quite straightforward, but this isn't always the case.

The subject you have in mind might be 'Life in Eighteenth-Century England' or 'Mythical Beasts Throughout The Ages'. These are such broad headings that, without a clear outline, set out in a logical order, you could end up in a terrible muddle.

In order to ensure that you are working logically, draft out a sensible framework in the form of a step-by-step outline. Discard anything that leads you away from the main theme, but retain the details for future use. One good, strong article can become the first of a series if you use the material wisely.

Before you begin, establish exactly which points you wish to cover, then place them in the sequence you feel is the most logical. For example, you may consider that chronological order would be the most sensible for an article on mythical beasts, so the sequence might be along the following lines:

1. the first recorded mythical creatures

2. the physical forms they have taken down the ages

3. examples of the forms in which various images have been represented, i.e. paintings, statues, etc.

4. examples of beasts which have a special religious significance

5. some twentieth-century equivalents.

Varying the format
The above sequence takes the reader logically through the subject and ties the ending up with the beginning by making a 'then and now' comparison.

You may feel, however, that a different order would be more appropriate. Perhaps you would prefer to concentrate on the artistic representations or religious significance. Another angle might be to compare each mythical beast with a possible real-life counterpart.

Whichever aspect you select, providing you stick firmly to the theme of the article and work towards bringing the ending back round to the beginning, you will achieve a satisfactory result.

WORKING TO A SET LENGTH

Writing for the mainstream press always involves writing to a set length. The publications all have:

- a set number of pages
- a predetermined amount of column inches
- a specific policy regarding illustrations
- a set format which is familiar to the readership.

Each article has to be designed to fit a specific slot within the magazine's format and the required information must be delivered within a predetermined number of words.

Specialising to start you off

The above rules always apply to mainstream titles, but there are a great many specialist and amateur publications which welcome articles from good freelance writers. Although many are restricted by cost to a limited number of pages, they can be far more flexible in the amount of space they are prepared to devote to a new contributor. The down side to this is that payment usually ranges from very low to non-existent, but for many new writers, simply seeing their 5,000 word article in print is sufficient reward.

By contrast, experienced freelances will invariably expect the full National Union of Journalists' (NUJ) rate per word for their contributions and they probably have a fair point. It is, however, worth bearing in mind that small circulation publications can sometimes prove extremely useful to the novice writer in providing both experience and a portfolio of published work.

Making it fit the space provided

Assuming that your article is for a mainstream publication, you must know the required number of words. If the
allotted space requires, say, 1,000 words, your article
should ideally be as close to that limit as possible,
somewhere between 900 and 1,100 words. Substantially
less or more than the given figure and the editor will have
their work cut out shaping the piece to fit its slot. At best,
your article will be cut to ribbons and at worst, the editor
will never use you again.

Turning the words around

When cutting a piece that is too long, it's a lovely but
misguided thought that all you have to do is simply
remove a few words here and there. Whilst you can
sometimes get away with cutting out a few chunks of
superfluous information, more often than not your best
course of action is to find a better way to use the few
words you have. This involves careful use of vocabulary,
turning words and phrases around so that the piece reads
more clearly, and never using two words when one will do.

See if you can cut the following piece without losing any of
the information it contains, rephrasing and altering the
vocabulary where necessary:

> I don't know about you but I love cats and I can't tell you
> how exciting I find the prospect of obtaining a new
> kitten. There are lots of things you have to remember to
> do before the kitten arrives. In the first place, you have to
> buy three dishes, one for water, which should have a
> solid base so that you can't upset it easily, one for food
> and one for milk. Oh, by the way, I should have

mentioned that the water must be cool and of course, it has to be clean and you should throw away stale water and refill the bowl with fresh water every day. (111 words)

Shortened rewrite at end of book page 225.

Assessing the length

Even in today's high-tech age of electronic word counts on PCs and word processors, many experienced writers still prefer to assess the length of a piece by the number of double-spaced typed A4 pages it covers. A very rough guide is that a double-line spaced A4 typewritten or word-processed page, with 3cm right- and left-hand margins, should amount to between 250 and 290 words.

Once you have established the word length per page, experience will eventually tell you when and where you need to start wrapping up the article you are writing.

Less is more

It is always far better to have too much material than too little. Write the piece to its natural length, then bring it down to the correct wordage by cutting out any superfluous words and detail.

If the article comes up too short, never be tempted to 'pad' it out with flowery description or irrelevant information. Re-read it to see if you've left anything out. If you can't find anything to fill the gap, then it may be that you don't have enough knowledge of your chosen topic to form the basis of an article. If this is the case, then put the idea aside until you have carried out more research and choose something else to write about.

CASE STUDIES

Sue tells you about herself

Sue is keen to write about her collection of antique china, but after typing out fifteen pages she can't think of anything more to write. Having given a rambling account of how she got started when a friend took her to a country house auction, she has run out of steam before giving any solid information about the antiques she collects.

Paul sets out the facts

Paul, a mechanic in his early fifties, is a vintage car enthusiast and has been involved in several restoration projects. He writes an article giving a step-by-step account of one such restoration, beginning with a brief history of the vehicle and ending with its modern equivalent. The finished article is accepted for publication in the specialist car magazine he has subscribed to for several years.

CHECKLIST

1. Does your article have an attention-grabbing opening?

2. Does your opening give a clear indication of what is to come?

3. Is the middle informative and interesting?

4. Does the ending tie up with the beginning?

5. Do you keep to the point from beginning to end?

ASSIGNMENT

Select a magazine which specialises in your subject area and see if you can write an article which will fit into its format and house style. Establish the required length by physically counting the words in articles published in the magazine.

Does your article have an attention-grabbing opening?

3

Getting Articles Into Print

WRITING FEATURES FOR MAGAZINES

Mainstream or specialist, the market for features is wide and varied. A feature article could be any one of the following:

- a 'think' piece commenting on an aspect of life relevant to your readership
- a 'reader's true story'
- a step-by-step 'how to' article
- a local or specialist interest piece
- an information piece, such as a travel article.

Freelancing as a professional

Taking the above examples one by one, 'think' pieces commenting on the idiosyncrasies of life in general are rarely written by unknown contributors.

This type of editorial tends to be staff-written either by a senior editor, professional journalist or well-known personality. However, a thought-provoking article on a topically controversial subject could find its way into print. Factual accuracy combined with real-life examples could be developed into a discussion feature, especially if it relates directly to the lives of the readers.

Features editor Clare Swatman of *Bella* magazine commissions discussion articles of this type for their **Reports** features. Whilst she welcomes subject ideas, these should be accompanied by an outline of how the feature would develop. Working knowledge of the magazine's style and format is essential if your suggestion is to be seriously considered.

Sinning, confessing and repenting

There are plenty of openings in the women's magazine market for readers' true tales, life-changing experiences, amazing escapes, daring feats of bravery and of course, the classic 'sin, confess and repent' stories which are an integral feature of many weekly magazines.

These personal interest stories are gleaned from a variety of sources:

- news agencies
- local newspapers
- help organisations
- sent in by readers.

Whilst some are pure sensationalism, most are designed to offer messages of hope to readers experiencing similar traumas in their lives.

Although many are staff-written, there are always openings for freelances who can write readers' true tales to a professional standard, but be aware when submitting your own personal confession story that, should it be accepted for publication, it will almost certainly be rewritten by a professional writer before it appears in print.

Sharing information

General information and 'how to' articles are perhaps marginally easier to place. The market for these is very wide and there is always room for the expert who can write clearly and informatively about his or her specialist subject.

Utilising local knowledge, arts and crafts

Regional publications are always on the lookout for specialist pieces with a local flavour, particularly if they highlight an item of unusual historical significance or are designed to publicise a forthcoming event.

Arts and craft articles will find a home not only in subject specific magazines, but also, where a thriving small business is concerned, in local newspapers and county magazines. Good subjects for such features would be designers and manufacturers of:

◆ hand-made pots
◆ quality furniture
◆ stained-glass windows
◆ novelty goods.

Finding a market

There are literally thousands of magazines currently on sale in the UK, only a small fraction of which are on display in newsagents and supermarkets. A large proportion of specialist publications have to be ordered or are obtained by subscription.

In addition to the well-known mainstream titles, listed below are just a few of the categories for specialist publications currently on the market.

- antiques
- brides and weddings
- business matters
- cars
- computers
- country matters
- environmental issues
- hair care and styling
- high fashion
- home improvement
- pets
- sport
- stamp collecting
- steam engines.

Playing the field

There simply isn't room in this book to list every single subject area, but in addition to the markets mentioned above, there is a less well-documented one in the form of magazines and newsletters produced by local schools, clubs, organisations and religious groups. Whilst they rarely offer any financial reward, these publications can provide a superb training ground for the new writer and lead them on to more lucrative opportunities.

Travelling and trekking

Travel articles range from short snippets about family day trips to thousands of words recounting the perils of backpacking through treacherous terrain in some far flung corner of the world.

When it comes to passing on your personal holiday experiences, whilst the backpacking one might be considered, consign the story of last year's package tour to Benidorm to the bin now, while you're ahead.

If you intend to write travel articles for publication, you will need at least some, if not all, of the following:

- knowledge of and contacts in the travel industry
- wide travelling experience
- current factual information about the holidays and locations you feature
- access to up-to-the-minute market information
- the ability to tailor the content and format to individual editorial requirements.

Although it is a specialist professional area, if you can fulfil the above criteria, then it is well worth giving travel writing a try. As with any other form of feature writing, there is always room for a fresh, new voice.

KNOWING YOUR SUBJECT

The advice to 'write about what you know' may appear to be rather obvious but in the world of the feature article, this may not be as straightforward as it seems.

Keeping up with the times

In order to write informative, factual articles, it is essential that you keep up with innovations in your chosen field. For example, your feature may be a relatively abstract one telling the story of how you coped with bereavement – a very personal experience which you hope will help your readers come to terms with a similar loss in their own lives. In addition to describing your own emotions, the article should also contain some or all of the following:

- useful advisory quotes from an acknowledged expert
- information about bereavement counselling services
- details on how to obtain financial help
- a book and leaflet list
- a list of useful contact addresses, websites, etc.

In the case of sudden avoidable death, details on how to recognise warning signs, preventative action and emergency first aid procedures should also be included.

Remember that the reason for writing an article is to inform the reader, so even a subject as painfully personal as this one must contain relevant, up-to-date, factual information.

USING PROFESSIONAL EXPERTISE

Taking the theme of writing about what you know one stage further, professional experts who can write with clarity about their subject are always in demand.

Establishing street cred

Providing you have the relevant credentials, there are always openings for writers who can translate technical information into terms the layman can understand. In some cases, the expert's first attempts at article writing may be in response to a request from an editor seeking material. Listed below are just a few examples of the type of magazines where this may occur:

- 'alternative' health therapies
- collectibles
- company 'in house'
- computer
- consumer
- electronic
- financial
- insurance
- legal
- medical
- scientific.

All of the above examples cover areas where the professional in their field can find their expertise in demand.

Cross-pollinating the markets

In a later chapter, we'll be looking at adapting your articles to suit different markets and if you study the list above, it soon becomes clear that a writer who is also, say, an experienced lawyer need not confine themselves purely to legal publications.

Perhaps the lawyer has a passion for a particular make of car – Morris Minor or Volkswagen Beetle for example. In addition to any features he or she may write about legal matters in general, there is also a clear possibility here for articles on a variety of law-related topics concerning car ownership and restoration. For example:

- your rights when buying and selling vehicles
- the law relating to roadworthiness
- the legal definition of 'vintage'
- laws governing the import and export of vehicles.

SHARING HOBBIES AND INTERESTS

You may not be a qualified professional but you may,

nevertheless, be an expert in your particular hobby. Indeed, sometimes the only difference between the gifted amateur and acknowledged professional is that the amateur is unpaid. Most enthusiasts subscribe to at least one magazine and many regularly write letters to the editor of their favourite publication.

Sharing hobbies and interests.

Taking the next step up the ladder

Once you've had a few letters published, there is no reason why you should not take the next step and submit an article. However, before you submit any completed articles, it is essential that you study your chosen market carefully to establish the sort of feature they are likely to publish.

Analysing the market

Whilst the articles described above would probably be most suitable for the smaller, specialist markets, some may also find a home in one of the many mainstream titles. Breaking into the major magazine market can be extremely difficult but fortunately, not impossible.

A quick scan of the listings in the *Writers' & Artists' Yearbook* (published by A & C Black) will reveal that few of the glossy monthlies are prepared to consider unsolicited manuscripts. Almost all of their material is either staff-written or commissioned from a pool of established freelances, usually well-known journalists or acknowledged experts in their particular field.

Diving into the pool

The situation with regard to women's weeklies and some of the smaller circulation specialist titles isn't quite so bad and currently, these offer some of the best opportunities for writers hoping to produce articles for the mass market readership.

If you intend to join the pool of established freelances, the first step is to choose a magazine which you particularly enjoy reading and analyse the format. Using Figure 3 as an example for the women's magazine market, you will find that a clear picture of the target readership will emerge. Whilst some of the categories will not apply, the analysis sheet can easily be adapted for specialist magazines.

Another specialist editor prepared to consider freelance submissions is John Lloyd of *Camping Magazine*. His comprehensive guidelines give details of his requirements for a range of features including equipment testing, travel, lifestyle and humour. He prefers would-be contributors to contact him first with their ideas and once again, the magazine analysis sheet applied in conjunction with his guidelines will provide a basis on which to draft your article outline.

Magazine title ....
Editor/editorial address ....
....
Cover price .... Weekly/monthly/quarterly/biannually/annually

Content	Number of columns/ pages	Average number of words per item	Staff-written*
Agony column			
Book/film/video reviews			
Celebrity interviews			
Competitions			
Crafts			
DIY			
Fashion			
Fiction			
Finance			
Food and drink			
Gardening			
Health and beauty			
Horoscopes			
Medical			
Motoring			
Patterns (knit/sew)			
Pets			
Readers' letters			
Readers' true life tales			
Special features			
Special offers			
The arts			
Travel			
Other (specify)			

TARGET GROUP ....

Fig. 3. Magazine analysis sheet (women's magazines).
*Editorial staff are usually listed on either first or last pages of the magazine.

PRODUCING MATERIAL FOR NEWSPAPERS

News articles or 'stories' for newspapers are almost always written by staff journalists or professional free-lances retained by the editor. It is, however, possible to write articles and occasional features for newspapers which have editorial space set aside for more general items. Some newspapers run occasional local interest features on topics such as:

◆ 'then and now' articles chronicling, for example, a lifetime working in local industry
◆ environmental and conservation projects
◆ historic buildings
◆ local history
◆ murders and haunted houses.

BECOMING A REGULAR COLUMNIST

A one-off feature of this type could well lead to a regular column. You may be asked to deputise for an existing columnist writing in a similar field of expertise or your features may prove so popular that the editor decides to offer you a regular slot.

In common with their magazine counterparts, many local newspapers carry some or all of the following editorial columns:

◆ crossword
◆ astronomy
◆ health
◆ gardening
◆ cookery
◆ competitions
◆ children's page
◆ legal
◆ motoring
◆ agony

- DIY
- financial
- fishing
- sport
- review (book, TV, film, CD, computer games theatre, etc.)
- travel.

Creating a niche

If the newspaper doesn't already have a column in your particular specialist field, it is always worth contacting the editor and suggesting that you write one for them. Bear in mind, however, that editorial space is at a premium in local newspapers and there simply may not be room for anything new.

In areas such as health, finance, gardening and DIY, short columns are often produced by major manufacturers in the various industries and circulated free of charge on a national basis.

As local newspaper budgets are very tight, an editor has to be convinced that paying you to produce a regular, personalised column is going to be more cost effective than reproducing one syndicated free to the newspaper.

Filling the space provided

Before you approach the editor, have in mind a clear format for your column and a list of topics to take you over a number of weeks. You will be allocated a set number of words and you will be expected to stick to this figure.

Add interest by including 'fillers' in the form of diagrams, photographs and snippets from company press releases, cutting or expanding your articles accordingly to meet the required wordage. Details on how to obtain these are given in Chapter 10 but initially, information will filter through from publicity mass mail shots to the media or from eagle-eyed public relations companies who pick up your column through cuttings services.

You will be given a 'lead time', a weekly deadline which will probably be around a fortnight before the publication date. It is useful to make a chart along the lines of the sample for a weekly DIY column in Figure 4, showing when and where each item should appear. Seasons must be taken into account, so you need to plan well ahead to ensure the right piece appears at the right time, filling in any blanks as soon as material is available.

Assuming that the first issue (week number 1) is scheduled for the first week in January, a draughtproofing article is ideal. The article will contain information on:

- the methods and products available
- preparation of surfaces
- the result you are aiming for.

A competition and photograph of the prize provides a filler for week 1, with the list of winners diaried forward providing another filler for week 5.

Stringing along

If you have a keen interest in local matters, you may be the ideal person to act as a **stringer** for your local newspaper. Having made yourself known to the editor

Week No.	Deadline date	Publication date	Topic	Additional items	Wordcount
1	19.12.0X	2.1.0Y	Draughtproofing your windows	Competitions – DIY quiz (closing date 12.1.0Y)	500+ product shot of prize
2	26.12.0X	9.1.0Y	Insulating your loft	Manufacturer's list of protective measures	500 + line drawings
3	2.1.0Y	16.1.0Y	Thawing frozen pipes	Manufacturer's safety instructions	400 + photo
4	9.1.0Y	23.1.0Y	Clearing sink blockages	Step-by-step diagrams	500+ line drawings
5	16.1.0Y	30.1.0Y		Answers to quiz List of winners	
6	23.1.0Y	6.2.0Y		DIY chain stores Valentine promo.	product shot
7	30.1.0Y	13.2.0Y	Making a bird nesting box (Valentine theme)		line drawings

Fig. 4. Sample planner for weekly DIY column.

through regular correspondence with the letters page or your own specialist column, he could ask you to become a 'stringer', keeping an eye out for any snippets of local news that you feel will be of interest and either writing them up yourself or passing them on to one of the staff journalists.

Writing for national daily papers

Whilst it is by no means impossible to write for the national dailies, it can be very difficult for an unknown writer to obtain a commission. However, one of the best ways of getting your foot in the door is to build up a large portfolio of cuttings of your published work.

Once you have an established track record for reliability and subject expertise in the local press, a national newspaper editor may be prepared to consider an occasional one-off feature, but be aware that you will be competing against a pool of very experienced professionals.

CASE STUDIES

Maureen tries her hand at travel writing

On her return from a thoroughly enjoyable package holiday in Greece, Maureen, a 30-year-old clerical worker, decides to write an article about her hilarious experiences at the hotel. Adding a word of warning about eating foreign food and family hotels full of shrieking children, she sends the article off to a women's magazine selected at random. It is returned with a standard rejection.

Josie runs a marathon

Recently recovered from a potentially life-threatening illness, 54-year-old Josie, a grandmother of six, is preparing to take part in her very first marathon with the intention of raising money for the hospital unit that saved her life. She contacts the editor of a women's magazine aimed at the over-forties and they ask to see an outline of an article about her experiences. The editor commissions her to write the article, suggesting Josie waits until she has run the marathon so that she can describe her emotions on achieving her goal. The article, illustrated with photographs taken by a staff photographer, is published three months later in the magazine.

CHECKLIST

1. Do you keep up to date with changes in your area of expertise?

2. Do you subscribe to a suitable trade journal?

3. Have you devised a forward planner for seasonal items?

4. Could you become a 'stringer' for your local newspaper?

5. Do you have additional skills you could apply to the content of the articles you write?

ASSIGNMENT

Take a selection of magazines in your chosen field of interest and apply the magazine analysis in Figure 3 to each of them in turn. Comparison of the results will give you a clear overview of the target readerships and the differences in format and style between each publication.

4

Researching and Filing Systems

GATHERING INFORMATION

You can never have enough information about your chosen topic. Whether or not you are an expert in your own field, research is vital.

Researching the subject

No matter how well you think know your subject, there are always gaps somewhere in your personal knowledge.

It is a brave writer who makes factual statements without any source material to back them up. Failure to provide this can result at best in a flood of letters from irate readers and at worst, never working for that editor again.

Always check your facts with at least three different sources. Opinions vary, theories are disproved and it is not uncommon to discover that methods you have been applying successfully for years are now hopelessly out of date.

It is also surprising how often something we are sure is accurate is actually totally incorrect. Checking my sources paid off for me when I wanted to use a quote I believed was attributed to Mark Twain. A visit to my local library failed to unearth the quote, so I contacted the county library's literary expert. He could find no evidence that Mark Twain ever said it and worse still, the quote itself appeared not to exist. To this day, I still don't know where I got it from.

Triple checking your facts

Fortunately, rather than disproving a long-held belief like the one above, triple-checking your facts usually helps you to confirm that your information is correct.

Researching an article on Halloween superstitions for a magazine aimed at the younger women's market, I discovered a recipe for conjuring up an apparition of one's future husband. I'd never heard of the superstition before, so I scanned several reference books and to my delight, found it was well-documented in all of them. The end result was a fun piece with a slightly risqué flavour, reviving an ancient custom on love and marriage.

Compiling a checklist

To ensure accuracy, before you complete the article, apply a checklist along the following lines:

◆ Have I made any statements which cannot be supported by a reputable source?

◆ Have I used the very latest information?

◆ Have I checked my facts against at least three sources?

◆ Have I double-checked all my figures and the wording of all my quotes?

◆ Are all quotes attributed to the correct sources?

Add your own checks to this list to ensure that the information contained in your articles is both current and accurate.

GAINING ACCESS TO REFERENCE MATERIAL

Joining a library
Enthusiasts invariably have extensive collections of books covering every aspect of their chosen field, from coffee table volumes comprising colour plates and little else, to complex technical manuals complete with blueprint diagrams.

However, no matter how many books we have on our specialist subject, there always comes a time when we need to track something down, cross reference or double-check our information, and the local library is an ideal source.

Making friends with your librarian
Librarians have a vast amount of expertise and will give you invaluable help and advice on where to locate the information you require.

Where your local branch is unable to help, you will be referred to the relevant person or to a specialist reference library. Some reference libraries levy charges or membership fees and you may have to provide proof of your identity and purpose to gain access.

You can obtain more information on this and other reference societies and organisations from the *Aslib Directory of Information Sources in the UK* which you can find in your local library.

Surfing the net

If you are already on the Internet, you will know all about the vast store of information you can now access through your computer.

Encyclopaedias, dictionaries and a wide variety of reference material are now available on CD-Rom and for those who cannot access the Internet at home, most central libraries are now on the Internet and the service is available free of charge.

ESTABLISHING CONTACTS

The more articles you write, the more adept you will become at locating and gathering reference material.

You will soon build up a network of contacts who can provide you with the information you require and, if necessary, pass you on to someone equally helpful.

Ideally, you should be regarding each topic from a variety of angles so that, whilst one source will help you with one article, the next will lead you down another, equally lucrative path.

Exploring unknown territory

For example, perhaps you are writing an article on local buildings of unusual architectural interest. In the course of your research, you come across someone who tells you that one of the buildings has a resident ghost and introduces you to a local historian. You now discover that several of your chosen properties are said to be haunted and learn the stories behind them.

Now comes a further revelation – the historian has heard that there have been some strange supernatural incidents in the stockroom of a modern high street chemist's shop. The pharmacist who suffered the experience agrees to see you and is, you discover in conversation, a soloist with the local choir.

You've never thought about the paranormal before or choral singing but a good article writer never wastes an opportunity and your research has led to you making a couple of very useful new contacts.

Beginning with your original idea, you now have several new opportunities for articles in different areas:

1. *TOPIC: Local buildings of architectural interest*
    (a) Architectural features.
    (b) The architects and planners behind each building.
    (c) The history of each building.
    (d) The background to each building and its influence on the area.
    (e) The occupants of each building.

(f) The story of some of the individuals who occupied the buildings.

2. *TOPIC: Haunted buildings in the area and their ghosts*
   (a) Haunted modern buildings in the area.
   (b) The background and story of individual ghosts.
   (c) Other supernatural experiences in the locality.
   (d) Historical tales about influential inhabitants in previous centuries.

3. *TOPIC: The background to and future of the local choir*
   (a) Taking part in recitals and choral competitions.
   (b) Being a chorister, experience, training, what it entails, etc.
   (c) An interview with the choirmaster.
   (d) Humorous incidents in the life of a chorister.

Knowing where to turn
The above examples are only a small sample of the articles which can mushroom from one basic idea.

As a bonus, not only do you have a variety of topics to write about, but you have also begun to establish a network of useful contacts. The advantages of knowing a local historian are obvious, but you also now have someone to turn to if you need technical advice not only on drugs and medicines, but also singing and music, in the shape of your spook-spotting, singing pharmacist.

ATTENDING LECTURES AND CONFERENCES
Whether amateur enthusiast or professional expert, there is bound to be an organisation devoted entirely to your area of interest.

Joining associations and societies

If you can, try to join at least one group and subscribe to at least one trade or specialist magazine. Many societies hold regular meetings and lectures and you should try to attend at least one a year. Where this is impossible, make sure you keep a close eye on any relevant literature that they send you. A well-organised group usually produces some form of newsletter or magazine which will keep you up to date with any changes, news and items of interest in your chosen area.

Listening to lectures

Lectures and conferences offer an ideal opportunity to make new contacts and gather the very latest information. Attendance costs can range from as little as a couple of pounds for association members to a couple of hundred pounds for a residential conference. However, in terms of updating and extending your knowledge, it is money well spent and costs can be offset against tax.

RECORDING AND STORING INFORMATION

Listed below are some minimum requirements for an article writer:

- various encyclopaedias and dictionaries
- a collection of both general and subject-specific reference books
- files of cuttings from newspapers, magazines, trade journals, etc.
- a notebook containing snippets of information (with the source and date noted)
- press release files

- magazine files
- a contact address book
- at least one directory of research sources
- access to the Internet
- a file of your own published articles.

Using the right equipment

You will also need suitable equipment on which to produce your manuscripts. Initially, you may consider that writing a monthly newsletter for your club hardly warrants the purchase of a typewriter, let alone a personal computer, but this view can be very short-sighted.

A typewritten manuscript is much easier to set out for duplication and more importantly, much easier to read. It also looks more professional and this will influence your approach to writing and make your article a more worthwhile proposition for the reader.

WP OR PC?

Although some of the smaller press magazines request that you submit your manuscripts on computer disk, the mainstream market still tends to prefer the initial approach to be on paper, either by fax or post. Once accepted, however, they could well ask you to supply the piece on disk or as an email attachment, and it is simply not financially viable to pay someone to do this for you.

Later on, we'll be looking at the impact of information technology (IT) on the freelance writer, but if you intend to produce articles on a regular basis, you would be advised to invest in a personal computer (PC) and get connected to the Internet as soon as you can.

Getting organised

For the computer literate, immediate transfer of every scribbled note of research and reference material onto suitably labelled floppy disks is the obvious step. For those who prefer a more traditional environment, sensibly labelled files are the answer. Whether electronic or manual, however, it is essential to devise a filing system that suits you.

For example, perhaps you write a DIY column. Initially, alphabetical order might seem the most obvious classification for filing your information, but as your files grow, things could become rather more complicated.

At first, it may seem sensible to file everything connected with, say, **W**allpaper under the letter **W**. Therefore, information about **W**all-stencilling would also be filed under **W**. OK so far, but where you would file additional stencilling information, about furniture or ceilings for example? Under **S** for Stencils, **F** for furniture, **C** for ceilings or **W** with the instructions for stencilling **W**alls?

Before long, you will have to devise a system of cross-referencing perhaps alphabetically, then by topic, then method and so on.

Accessing the information

Whilst computers have revolutionised the way we store, maintain and retrieve information, they are vulnerable to power cuts, viruses etc. and it is, therefore, essential to have a back-up system in place. Vital information should always be copied to disks, which can then be colour coded for easy storage and retrieval. You may also find it useful to complement any electronic methods with a tried and tested paper-based system.

For the sake of speed, card indexes are still a very useful method of cataloguing and locating things quickly, and there are advantages to be gained from having the information to hand on paper in a colour-coded, numbered file.

It is up to the individual writer to choose their preferred method, bearing in mind that the more comfortable you are with a system, the more organised and easier it will be to lay your hands on the information you require.

UPDATING YOUR RECORDS

Try to keep your records as up to date as possible. People have a tendency to move on, so contact names and telephone numbers will change from time to time.

Clearing out old material

Whenever possible, take the time to go through your files and clear out any obsolete material. Organisations are tending to revamp their images more frequently nowadays and societies have a habit of changing their names. New technology is also impacting in all kinds of ways, so regular clearouts are vital to avoid confusion. Do take care, however, not to destroy anything that might turn out to be useful. If in doubt, rather than throw it out, the wary article writer will hang onto it, however dubious it might be.

CASE STUDIES

Bill gets egg on his face

Bill's local history article has been published in his parish magazine. The piece concerns the background to an area of common land, known locally as 'Drake's Run'. Basing his article on an old folktale his gran told him about the land being named after Sir Francis Drake, Bill fails to check his facts. Shortly after the article is published, the local vicar receives dozens of letters from his parishioners informing him that the name originated from the now defunct practice of driving flocks of ducks across the land to market.

Terry sets up a system

Having sold several articles to specialist magazines, Terry, a retired accountant, sets up a system of cross-referencing, storage and retrieval on his personal computer and compiles a list of suitable markets for articles, detailing the editorial requirements for each individual magazine. He now has easy access to accurate information for a variety of articles and markets.

CHECKLIST

1. Do you have a filing system in place?

2. Are your paper files and computer disks clearly labelled?

3. Are you a member of a professional/trade association?

4. Do you have a supply of reference books?

5. Do you have your own personal directory of contacts?

ASSIGNMENT

Select a topic and write down as many facts about it off the top of your head as you can. Now check each fact in turn from the information you have in your home. Did you get your facts right? If the answer is 'no', do not attempt to write an article until you have updated all the relevant information. If 'yes' did you discover anything new you could add to your article?

Do you have a filing system in place?

5

Rewriting to Suit Different Markets

One of the advantages of article writing is that the same information can be utilised again and again, providing it is written to the editorial style of each individual publication.

ADAPTING YOUR STYLE

Depending on the slot you are writing for, there may also be scope to vary your style to suit the topic you are writing about. For example, the following extracts are taken from two articles I wrote for a newspaper column I produced for teenagers.

Extract 1

If you need some extra cash to see you through further education courses, it's not too difficult to find yourself a summer job. Depending on your age and qualifications, there is a wealth of opportunity to not only earn money but also gain experience for your future career.

Extract 2

My sister had done it again. She'd been over my things without asking permission and had borrowed the black skirt I wanted to wear for a special date. I stormed into her room in a fury, 'I'll give you five seconds to give me back my skirt,' I shook my fist at the relaxed figure lying on the bed, 'or I won't be responsible for my actions.'

The first example is purely factual, setting out holiday job opportunities for students. The second, whilst it is factually accurate, is a light-hearted approach to coping with stress.

Respecting the reader

When I was asked to write the column, I knew how important it was not to patronise my teenage readers.

With straight information pieces like the student holiday one, I stuck to a standard factual format, but for others, I decided that the best way to achieve reader identification was to invent a younger sister who would invariably get the better of me.

By the end of the two years in which I produced the column, I had created a complete cast of fictional characters to portray the factual situations I wrote about each week. Through the story-telling quality provided by the dialogue and interaction between the characters, I was able to tackle topics as serious as drug-taking without preaching or talking down to my readership.

Wearing different hats

You should be prepared to change your writing style to suit not only the topics you are covering but also the readership of each individual publication.

Read the magazines and newspapers you intend to write for and get to know their formats inside out. Subscribe to them for several months and try to absorb the style and feel of the editorial and feature articles.

Take a simple theme and write a paragraph about it. The example below tackles hygiene in the kitchen, beginning by explaining the correct method of washing your hands before preparing food.

> Before you touch any food, wash your hands thoroughly. Fill the sink with water. Take a bar of soap and with your hands in the water rub the soap in between your palms to work up a lather. Make sure you clean in between your fingers and use a nailbrush to scrub any dirt from under your nails. When you have finished, rinse off the soap and dry your hands on a clean towel.

Now rewrite this or your own passage in the editorial style of any one or all of the following publications:

- a magazine aimed at young, single women
- a magazine aimed at mature women
- a cookery magazine
- a food industry leaflet
- a handbook for canteen staff
- a children's cookery column
- your local newspaper
- a quality national newspaper
- a tabloid newspaper
- a humorous, personal experience article.

ALTERING THE ANGLE

Different markets demand a different approach, so you will have to adapt the format accordingly.

Knowing where to put the emphasis

Returning to the above list, a leaflet for the food industry would probably take the form of a step-by-step guide to cleanliness in the kitchen. For a tabloid newspaper, the handwashing part of the article would be a tiny section in a shock piece on poor hygiene in the average home.

Whilst both articles would tackle the link between unwashed hands and food contamination, in the industry leaflet the emphasis would be on the correct procedure to minimise the chance of infection. In the tabloid piece, the emphasis would be on true life horror stories of people contracting life-threatening illnesses from eating contaminated food.

MAKING THEM LAUGH

Humour is a very powerful tool in getting a message over to a reader. Everyone enjoys a good laugh and a piece describing the disastrous attempts of the writer to achieve their goal can not only entertain but also inform.

Laughing at yourself

Unfortunately, it is extremely difficult to make people laugh, and unless it comes naturally to you, it is best avoided. However, well-written humour hugely increases your chances of a sale, so providing you have the ability to laugh at yourself, you may strike gold. When writing humour, bear in mind the following points:

- The reader must be able to identify with the situation you are describing.

- You must have an empathy with the reader.

- Avoid making fun of anyone but yourself.

- Use the word 'you' as much as possible.

- Be prepared to be the 'fall guy', making yourself the butt of any jokes.

- Never appear so stupid that the reader will be contemptuous of you.

- Take the 'everyman' role, so that you establish an immediate link with the reader.

Your aim is to have the reader laughing with, not at, you. They should be able to immediately recognise the people and situations you are describing and relate to your situation sympathetically.

Sending up familiar situations

When writing for a specialist market, you have the advantage of being able to use so-called 'in-house' humour. This is where you are writing about a profession, hobby or lifestyle that you share with your readership. You could, for example, write humorous pieces on your disastrous first attempts in any of the following fields:

- amateur photography
- camping
- DIY
- oil painting
- sailing
- sport

and so on. Many of your readers will have made similar mistakes to the ones you are describing and an instant empathy will be established between you.

Alternatively, you may be writing for a national market, where your readers would relate to day-to-day situations such as:

- assembling a flatpacked piece of furniture
- high street shopping with a double buggy
- holiday packing for a family of four
- how to survive building an extension to your house.

Laughing at work and play

One of the advantages of writing for publications such as your club or firm's magazine is that you have immediate reader identification with the situations and events you are describing. Your readers will already have a rapport with you and it will be much easier to make them laugh about situations in which they have been personally involved.

TAKING PHOTOGRAPHS

Photographs not only offer a visual dimension to your articles but may also attract an extra fee. Black and white photographs are still widely used, although colour transparencies are usually acceptable. Take several pictures of your subject from a variety of angles and select the ones that best illustrate the piece you are writing.

Developing your film

No matter how fond you are of your battered old Brownie, if you intend to submit photographs to illustrate your article, use a good camera. Modern cameras do almost all the focusing and winding on for you, so there is no excuse for submitting photos with fuzzy images or double exposures.

You will need to use a specialist photography shop to develop your black and white film. Ask for a 'contact sheet' – your set of photographs printed on one sheet – from which you can select the clearest and most effective prints.

Employing professional photographers

Many magazines employ their own staff photographers or commission freelances to illustrate your article for you.

Bella, for example, send along their own photographer to take the pictures of the people and homes which accompany their 'true-life' features.

In some cases, you may have a professional contact of your own whom you can suggest to an editor, although you will lose out on any fee for illustrations.

You can also obtain photographs from picture libraries, but you will have to pay for this service. Fortunately, photographs and colour slides that arrive attached to press releases are intended for publication and you can use these free of charge. PR companies will, however, expect you to return transparencies after use.

Captioning and cross-referencing photographs

Every photograph you submit will need a caption, and you must make it clear to the editor exactly which section of the text it refers to. Perhaps the simplest method is to number each photograph, annotating your manuscript accordingly as shown in Figure 5.

Fig 5. Photograph of Lavenham Church, Suffolk
(*reproduced courtesy of Linda Sutton*)
Annotate photographs within the text of your article, numbering them
consecutively for easy identification, e.g. '...our tour of the area ended
with a visit to Lavenham Church (pic 3). This superb example of...'

Fixing the captions

Put your name, address and telephone number on the
back of the photograph either lightly in pencil or
preferably printed on a small adhesive label. Never
write in ink as this will show through and can spoil the
surface.

Numbered captions should be typed on adhesive labels
and fixed to the back of the relevant photo. For colour
slides, place each transparency inside an envelope with
the caption typed on it.

Brushing up your camera techniques

Because photographs often attract an extra fee, it is
worth brushing up on your camera technique and
ensuring that you supply good, clear photographs.

The copyright in a photograph belongs, initially, to the person who takes the picture, so in theory, they can be used again and again. However, if you intend to rewrite your article for several different markets, bear in mind that the pictures must be tailored to suit the various formats. Photographs should be:

- numbered and have captions which relate to the text
- sharp and clear
- trimmed to fit the allotted space
- well-balanced so that the subject is clearly framed by the background.

Copyright in any photographs you take should remain with you so you must ensure that you are informed, in writing, of the copyright you have sold and whether or not you are at liberty to sell the photograph on elsewhere.

QUOTING THE EXPERTS

There is no copyright on fact, only in the form of words that is used. If, for example, I state that any change in your life, no matter whether it is good or bad, will cause you some inconvenience, this could be said to be a statement of fact.

Alternatively, I could use the following quote, 'Change is not made without inconvenience, even from worse to better,' Samuel Johnson (*A Dictionary of the English Language*).

Scanning the page, you can see the difference in the way that the two statements are laid out. The first is indistinguishable from the body of the text, the other is set within speech marks and credited to the person who first said it.

Crediting your source

You should always state the source of any quotations that you use. When writing instructional articles, you will need to refer to and quote from standard textbooks in order to establish credibility and subject knowledge.

In more light-hearted articles, you may wish to use well-known quotations to illustrate your point. In both cases, you should double-check the wording in order to avoid misquoting the source.

Infringing copyright

According to the *Writers' & Artists' Yearbook* (A & C Black), you can 'quote up to 200 words for the purpose of criticism or review'. For any other purpose or larger sections, you should seek permission from the publisher of the work.

However, even for very short passages, crediting the source of a quotation not only reinforces your subject expertise to the reader but is also a matter of common courtesy to your fellow professionals. Treat them courteously in the first instance and they will be only too pleased to give you further help whenever the need arises.

CONDUCTING INTERVIEWS

A good interviewer is a person who is outgoing, friendly and genuinely enjoys meeting new people.

Who do you interview?

As far as the media is concerned, the ideal interviewee is someone everyone wants to read about. The sole survivor of a major air disaster, the victor in a multi-million pound libel action, the spouse of a tragic murder victim.

However, the people involved in these and similar national news items will invariably be inaccessible to the average freelance writer. Those who decline to sign an exclusive contract immediately with a national newspaper, magazine or publicist will usually be snapped up by professional journalists working for international news agencies. The interviews will be syndicated to the media in the UK and abroad until interest wanes and the income runs dry.

There is, nevertheless, plenty of opportunity for you to place well-written interviews with people likely to be of interest to a specific readership, providing the content is topical.

Looking for an angle

If you intend to write celebrity interviews for publication, then you must be aware of the media's attitude towards them. Provided your interviewee is currently in the public eye, your interview will be saleable. If not, then no matter how famous they used to be, no editor will be interested in publishing the piece.

Whether or not your subject is in the public eye, an interview is rarely solely about the interviewee. It also serves to inform the reader about a particular item of interest. In order to catch the eye of an editor, the people you interview should be currently engaged in a new project. They may, for example:

◆ have just written a book, made a record, TV programme or film
◆ have invented a revolutionary new process
◆ be in the process of achieving success in an area entirely new to them
◆ be the first or last person to have been involved in an event of current national interest.

Hanging it on a hook

Where you are featuring professional experts, rather than well-known media personalities, you need to find a 'hook' on which to hang your article. For example, for an interview aimed at a magazine for photography enthusiasts, the interviewee could be:

◆ a photographer (amateur or professional) who captured an historic incident on film
◆ a person who devised a revolutionary innovation in camera design
◆ a photographer (amateur or professional) who produces specialist pictures – nature, portraits, wide-angled, sport, etc.

An interview featuring any of the above subjects is unlikely to stand on its own. In order to make it publishable, it will have to be linked with a current event. The anniversary of the historic incident, for example, a much improved version of the camera's design change, or an exhibition of the photographer's work.

Keep an eye out for anniversaries. People who were in on the beginning of a brand new process or invention planning to celebrate its twenty-fifth year in commercial use are ideal for this purpose. Always look for an angle and seek out ordinary people who have done extraordinary things.

Preparing beforehand

In order to conduct a successful interview, you must be prepared by ensuring that you have all of the following:

◆ prior knowledge of the interviewee and their area of expertise
◆ a prepared list of questions
◆ an appointment
◆ the ability to listen.

Asking the right questions

The questions you ask will depend very much on the type of article you are writing. If it is aimed at a women's magazine, then the emphasis will be on the person's background, home and family.

If it is for a specialist hobby or professional publication, the emphasis will be on subject expertise. As a rough guide, a good interview should contain:

◆ a brief physical description of the interviewee
◆ a brief description of your surroundings
◆ factual information about the person's area of expertise
◆ some background information about the person

- a little about how they envisage their future or the development of their project
- a list of useful addresses where you can obtain further information.

An optional extra is a photograph of the person, their surroundings and/or workplace and/or the equipment they use.

Having a friendly chat

It pays to let the interviewee do all the talking. The more you take the role of fascinated listener, the more they will tell you about themselves.

Try to avoid asking **closed** questions. These are questions to which the answer can be either 'yes' or 'no'. For example:

- Do you enjoy your job?
- Is the equipment complicated to use?
- Are you planning to marry in the foreseeable future?

Faced with a shy or, indeed, hardened interviewee, the above questions will be useless in obtaining the replies you are after. Always ask **open** questions, ones that will encourage your interviewees to talk about themselves:

- What is it about your job that gives you most satisfaction?
- The equipment looks rather complicated. How can a layman use it?
- You've been with your partner for some time now.

How do you see your future together?

Listing dates and checking your facts

List any dates you are given and double-check them before you leave. You may prefer to make a recording of the conversation, but be aware that many people find having their conversation taped intrusive and possibly intimidating.

If you genuinely find it difficult to make comprehensive notes during an interview, ask permission to tape it. Use a machine with a built-in microphone as this is less intrusive and you avoid problems with setting it up correctly.

Some interviewees will have press photos you can use to accompany the article. If not, ask before you take photographs – never just snap away without permission.

Being trustworthy

It is vital that you prove you can be trusted. If your interviewee has confided in you, don't break their confidence or they will spread the word and you'll find other people will be reluctant to speak to you.

If the interviewee made you welcome, write and thank them for their hospitality and always check your copy with them before submitting it to the editor. Sensational 'inside stories' are best left to the tabloid journalists. If you want to write regularly for the less controversial markets, build up a reputation of trust and accuracy and you will find yourself in great demand.

Interviewing styles

Interviews are conducted and written up in a variety of styles, depending upon the preference of the writer and the format of the magazine. An interview may be:

- straightforward question and answer (Q & A)
- a cosy chat using direct speech
- an article on a specific topic, using snatches of Q & A dialogue to explain technical information
- a representation of the interviewee as seen through the eyes of the interviewer
- a comparison of three different people's experiences, one good, one bad, one balancing the other two.

Giving the reader what they want

A good interview is one in which the questions elicit the answers everyone, i.e. your readers, want to hear. Experienced interviewees will be skilled in avoiding revealing the things they don't want you to know. Inexperienced subjects may have difficulty giving you the answers you require. It is up to you to ask the right questions and interpret the answers correctly and in a manner that will inform and hold the reader through to the end.

CASE STUDIES

Pam goes back to school

Pam, a keen letter writer to magazines and newspapers, learns that one of her neighbours was the last headteacher of the long-closed village school. She conducts a lengthy interview with her and sends it to the editor of her local newspaper. It is returned with a brief note explaining that as the school closed so long ago, the interview has no topical interest for their readers.

Sandra finds a hook

Sandra, a member of a writers' circle, is collecting her child benefit at the post office when she sees an actor from a now-defunct television series. Eavesdropping on the conversation with the counter clerk, Sandra discovers that the actor is an expert cactus grower who has taken time out from acting to write a book on his horticultural activities. He is happy to give her an interview, which she sells to the local newspaper to appear in time to coincide with the publication of his book.

CHECKLIST

1. Can you rewrite your article to suit several different markets?

2. Are all quotes credited to the correct sources?

3. Is your article topical?

4. Will the humour appeal to a sufficiently wide readership?

5. Is your interview with someone currently in the public eye?

ASSIGNMENT

Choose someone, either alive or dead, whom you would love to interview and compile a list of questions you would like to ask them. Ask a friend to assume the role of interviewee and see if your questions elicit the answers you expected.

6

Writing Short Stories

UNDERSTANDING THE MARKET

In the previous chapters, we looked at the disciplines involved in writing factual articles for publication.

For many would-be fiction writers, keen to see their literary masterpieces in print, it can be quite a shock to discover that not only do exactly the same disciplines apply but that there are far fewer openings for short stories than there are for non-fiction articles.

Sadly, the scarcity of short story markets is not confined to magazines. Fewer mainstream publishers than ever before are prepared to consider single author short story collections, prompting writers to turn to small independents and self publishing in an attempt to bring their anthologies into the market place. Unfortunately, this may not be the most practical solution, as it is relatively difficult to persuade high street retailers to stock independently produced books.

At the time of writing, the Arts Council England is running a 'Save Our Short Story' campaign aimed at combating discrimination against the short story form within the mainstream publishing industry. Their initial research has revealed that, despite the growing number of independently published anthologies, virtually all of the year's top 100 short story bestsellers were written by established novelists and published by mainstream publishers.

Defining the short story

A short story may be defined as a work of fiction not exceeding 10,000 words in length. However, the market for 10,000-word stories is so limited as to be almost non-existent. The best hope of seeing your stories in print is to aim them at specific magazines who you know publish the sort of story you enjoy writing.

The market for short stories falls into two main categories:

1. genre publications i.e. Horror, Fantasy, Science Fiction (SF), Crime and Romance
2. women's magazines.

There are also a number of literary outlets which will consider fiction from new writers.

Getting paid for your stories

As far as genre publications are concerned, the good news is that they may be willing to publish much longer stories than those featured in women's magazines. Some might even accept stories of up to and over 8,000 words.

The bad news is that payment rates are often very low and in some cases, non-existent.

Playing fair with the writer

This is not a deliberate attempt to defraud the writer, simply a question of basic economics.

Magazine production costs are relatively high and editors have to economise somewhere. A large proportion of genre magazines are produced by small presses, fan clubs and writers' groups or are imported from overseas. They may be available only on subscription and have fairly low circulation figures. Reputable editors will do their best to pay their contributors a basic fee and should profits begin to rise, will try to increase payment rates accordingly.

Provided you find an editor who will play fair with you, these markets can offer a reputable route to publication for a host of budding genre fiction authors.

The same is true of literary publications, many of which are produced by legitimate writing organisations. In common with the genre magazines, whilst financial rewards may be scant, the good ones offer a useful showcase for new writing talent.

Mslexia, for example, welcomes well-written and well-formed contemporary fiction, but currently does not have sufficient funds to pay for fiction manuscripts. However, the stories published in the magazine stand an excellent chance of being read by agents, publishers and fellow practitioners.

Perhaps the best known media outlet for literary short stories is the fifteen minute daily BBC Radio 4 slot.

Although most of the stories are commissioned, unsolicited manuscripts from unpublished authors are considered.

Steering clear of vanity publishers

When scanning national newspapers for possible markets, steer well clear of any advertisements offering publication of your short stories in an anthology. These are nothing more than con tricks on the part of greedy vanity publishers and work along the same lines as their better-publicised counterparts operating in the poetry world.

Readers are invited to submit their stories, often as competition entries. They then receive a letter singing their praises, with the promise of publication in the next edition of the publisher's anthology. The author is subsequently invited to purchase the anthology for a knock-down price and, inspired by success, is usually unable to resist the temptation to order not just one but several more copies to distribute among family and friends.

Sadly, this will be just about as wide as the distribution network gets. Volumes produced by the vanity press are invariably poorly produced and unsaleable to reputable retail outlets.

It is, in fact, incredibly difficult to get an anthology of short stories accepted for publication by a genuine publishing house. The few that are published are designed to fit into set categories and of these, the majority are collections of stories by several well-known authors in a specific field – horror, crime or ghost stories, for example, preferably by long-dead authors whose works are out of copyright and therefore, economical to reprint.

A small number of anthologies feature stories by one highly saleable author on a set theme, and other selections can be found in specialist areas such as gay or lesbian fiction, ethnic stories and feminist issues.

For writers tempted by dreams of stardom to part with their hard-earned cash, the following rule applies equally to poetry, autobiographies, novels and short stories:

PUBLISHERS PAY YOU

Treat any advertisements offering to publish an anthology of your work with extreme caution, and if anyone asks you for money, grab your manuscripts and run as fast as you can in the opposite direction.

Writing for women's magazines

For those authors who wish to write short fiction for the mass market, women's weekly magazines are almost the only outlet accessible to them.

Whilst there are one or two fiction opportunities in women's monthly magazines, they are limited. The bulk of the material featured in the monthlies is either staff-written, commissioned from well-known authors or extracts from or serialisations of published novels.

The fiction pages of women's weeklies are more accessible to freelance contributors than their monthly counterparts. The stories may have few literary pretensions but they nevertheless entertain millions of readers every week. Fees vary across the industry but you are not expected to produce material without payment and you will have the satisfaction of seeing your work regularly on sale in newsagents nationwide.

ANALYSING PUBLISHED FICTION

The one thing you cannot do if you want to see your fiction published in a women's magazine is send the editor any story of any length, style or genre you choose.

Knowing who publishes what

Each magazine has its own format, tone, style and target readership. Before you send your manuscript off, you must know you are aiming it in the right direction.

Choose a selection of magazines which you enjoy reading and study them from cover to cover. There will usually be a note on an editorial page either at the beginning or end of the magazine, stating whether or not the editor is prepared to consider stories submitted 'on spec'.

Please heed warnings stating that 'we do not consider unsolicited manuscripts'. Ignoring them is pointless and in order to push this point home, some editors add a further deterrent in the form of a disclaimer concerning the safe return of unsolicited material.

If there is no indication in the magazine, check in the *Writers' & Artists' Yearbook* or telephone the magazine's editorial department to ask whether they are prepared to

Magazine ....

Fiction editor* ....

Editorial address ....

....

.... Tel: ....

....

Type of fiction	**No. of words**
Romance	....
Lifestyle	....
Twist-in-the-tale	....
Serial	....
Other (specify)	....

Approx. age of characters......................................

Occupations ....

Theme of story ....

Vocabulary (formal, slang, etc.) ....

Style (gentle, tough, etc.) ....

Fig. 6. Story analysis form.
*Editorial staff are usually listed either on the first or last pages
of the magazine.

read stories submitted 'on spec' and to establish the name of the fiction editor.

Use the magazine analysis form (Figure 3) to determine the format, tone and target readership of your chosen publications, then apply the story analysis form in Figure 6 to the fiction in each magazine.

From your research, you will discover that the proportion of fiction varies enormously from one magazine to another.

The changing face of fiction

Most feature only one very short story, between 850 and 1,200 words and often with a surprise or twist ending. Others have as many as three or four complete stories and a romantic serial but these are the exception rather than the rule.

If you are one of the many writers who cut your teeth on the short stories in your mother or grandmother's weekly magazines, reading a current issue of *Woman* or *Woman's Own* can be something of a culture shock. Over the past ten years or so, the influence of the German publishing industry on the UK market has made a profound difference to the format and style of women's weeklies.

The introduction of titles such as *Bella* and *Best* in the 1980s took the industry by storm and opened the way for others in their mould. Meanwhile, in an effort to combat falling circulation figures as their readership transferred its affections to the new style magazines, old faithfuls such as *Woman* and *Woman's Own* began to update their image.

As a result, the tone, format and length of magazine fiction has changed dramatically from the days when you had at least one complete romantic story and a serial to get your teeth into each week.

RELATING TO THE READERSHIP

In order to understand why the German magazines knocked their UK counterparts off their perches, you need to be aware of who actually reads the stories you wish to write.

Looking at their faces

One of the advantages of the new style magazines is the number of 'true-life tales' they feature, accompanied by photographs of the people involved.

Look at their faces, study the articles and familiarise yourself with their lifestyles. Perhaps the most notable changes have been in the attitude towards single and working mothers.

A large proportion of the women featured are lone parents, and as so many mothers go out to work, the pace at which they live their lives has increased enormously. Stay-at-home mums preoccupied with housework, cooking and child-rearing are no longer the target readership.

For today's modern reader, cleaning the house is a necessary evil, convenience foods are the norm and their children attend playgroups or nurseries, or are cared for by childminders.

Look closely too at the differences between age and social groups. In magazines carefully targeted at younger women, the vocabulary, attitudes and behaviour will be very different from that reflected in magazines designed to appeal to the over-fifties.

Paying attention to the advertisements

Study the advertisements in your chosen publications. What sort of products are they selling?

Look, too, at the cookery, fashion, beauty and health pages. You will find that, in magazines aimed primarily at young mums, many of the products featured are linked to leading catalogue companies and major chain stores.

For older readers, the emphasis is on health products, stair lifts, support hose and foot warmers.

Empathising with the reader

If, when you read the magazine, you find that you cannot relate to the characters in the stories or the people in the true-life features, try another market for your work.

You will not, through your fiction, make your readers rethink their attitudes, bring them to a higher intellectual plane or encourage them to be interested in people whose lives have no relevance whatsoever to their own.

Magazine short stories are 'quick-fix' entertainment. If you would really like to give it a try but are not quite sure whether a particular magazine is right for you, a glance through the letters pages should clinch it for you.

Sharing experiences

The letters will contain anecdotes, family stories, tips and comments which you instantly recognise and hopefully relate to. They might cover any or a mixture of the following:

- an amusing story about a grandchild
- a complaint about lack of facilities in shops for mums with pushchairs

- ◆ a middle-aged mother's thwarted attempt to return to the workplace
- ◆ retraining after redundancy
- ◆ the hopelessness of being a young jobless person
- ◆ an account of an amusing incident at home or in the workplace
- ◆ the joys of being a parent
- ◆ a gripe about rude shop assistants or offensive customers.

The subjects chosen will give you a clear indication of the age range of your readership, the things that interest them and the vocabulary they use.

Writing about real people

Whichever publications you attempt to write for, you must write about people to whom the readership can relate. They must be instantly recognisable and, within the confines of your fictional story, the backgrounds, settings and situations must be as real as you can possibly make them.

Magazine fiction is character-driven, which means that the emphasis must be on the characters rather than the settings, which should simply serve to enhance the characterisation.

Escaping into make-believe

The amount of truly escapist fiction in women's magazines is surprisingly small. There are one or two publications which still feature traditional 'boy meets girl' and historical romances, but these are the exception.

In the main, modern magazines are looking for modern attitudes and situations in their storylines. The story's characters must reflect the age range of the readership and the relationships must reflect today's society, whether the story involves coping with early retirement or having your central character agonising over whether she should commit herself to marriage with her long-term lover.

EXPLORING YOUR OPTIONS

The type of story you write will depend on what gives you the most pleasure and the format of the magazine at which you are aiming your manuscripts.

Sending a tough twist-ender to a magazine which you know only publishes gentle romance is a total waste of effort. Get to know your chosen markets inside out over a period of months, until you reach the point when you can be reasonably confident that your story does fit into the right fiction category.

Categorising short stories

Remember that modern readers live hectic lives. Magazine stories tend to be categorised under titles such as:

- 3-Minute Fiction
- Quick Read
- Coffee Break Fiction
- Story on a Page.

One magazine, which used to describe its stories as 'heartwarming', 'sensitive' and 'moving', now simply publishes fiction under the heading 'short story'. This alone demonstrates the change in emphasis for today's busy reader.

As detailed in the story analysis form, there are four main types of magazine fiction:

1. Romance
2. Twist-in-the-Tale
3. Lifestyle
4. Serials.

Romances are tales of love and hope for the future. They may not be quite the standard 'boy meets girl' format, but the characters do fall in love and for the most part, there is the promise that they will live happily ever after.

Twist/surprise endings
Stories with a twist or surprise ending, originally rather hard-edged when introduced by the German magazines, have been gradually softening over the intervening years in response to the need of the readership for uplifting stories which, for a brief moment, will take them away from the less pleasant aspects of their daily lives.

The advantage of the twist-in-the-tale format is that the stories fall into almost any genre, from romance to murder mystery. *Bella* magazine will even consider science fiction twists providing they fit the magazine's format, offering a lone outlet for this specialised genre within the women's magazine market.

Coping with everyday situations

Lifestyle stories have, in some cases, replaced the standard romance. In these stories, the characters deal with the sort of problems that the readership will understand and immediately relate to. Topics such as:

◆ taking a long, hard look at their marriage
◆ struggling with the role of step-parent
◆ overcoming a teenage child's hostility
◆ rebuilding life after a broken romance
◆ forming relationships as the parent of a disabled child
◆ rethinking attitudes within a relationship and meeting others halfway
◆ facing and coping with a new way of life.

Serialising your story

Magazines like *Woman's Weekly* and *My Weekly* do still take serials, although a large proportion are adaptations of published novels.

There is, nevertheless, always room for a good writer who can break their stories down into bite-sized chunks that will appeal to the magazine's readership. Serials also form one of the few categories in which historical romance still features.

Fitting into other categories

In order to have the best chance of acceptance, the wise fiction writer will produce stories with a specific magazine slot in mind.

However, every now and then, a new opportunity arises and you may just be lucky enough to be in the right place at the right time. Whilst it is extremely rare for an editor to be so taken with a manuscript that falls outside their usual format that it will be accepted for publication, the inspired opportunist can occasionally strike lucky.

For example, a growing number of titles are supplementing their weekly editions with regular 'fiction specials'. Whilst still carefully targeted at a specific audience, the featured stories vary considerably in length and style, offering a potential market for all those previously hard-to-place manuscripts clogging up your files.

Hitting the holiday season

It is not unusual for a major magazine to bring out a Summer or Winter Special or a 'library' edition – a collection of stories previously published in the magazine. At Christmas time, a magazine may also bring out a double-issue to take them over the holiday period.

There are also certain times of the year, particularly during holiday seasons, when editors can find themselves short of material to fill their pages. It is at these times that they may be prepared to consider using a longer piece than usual or something with a slightly different slant.

Taking something from the 'slush' pile

It is very rare indeed for this type of fiction to be taken from the stack of unsolicited manuscripts, commonly referred to as the 'slush' pile, that clutter the desks of all magazine fiction editors. Editors seeking something new or stories to make up a special edition will usually make direct contact with writers with a proven track record to ask if they can provide them with anything suitable. Such an approach from an editor should never be seen as a commission. A commissioned piece is one where there is a written agreement regarding format and payment between the editor and the writer before a manuscript is produced.

A telephoned request for sample stories is only one stage up from sending your work 'on spec'. The editor is quite entitled to return your manuscripts as unsuitable and you have to take that decision on the chin. The fact that you were approached at all is an excellent sign that the editor has faith in your ability and is keen to use your work.

FOLLOWING THE GUIDELINES

We'll be looking at lengths and formats for the above magazine fiction categories in Chapter 8, but by far the best way to find out what they want is to read the magazines and familiarise yourself with the type of stories they publish.

Editors who are prepared to consider unsolicited manuscripts will usually issue editorial guidelines which will give you an idea of the sort of thing they are looking for. However, be aware that these are only a guide. They will not tell you how to write the stories and they are regularly updated. When you send off for guidelines, remember to include a stamped self-addressed envelope or you will not receive a reply.

Giving the editors what they want

The feedback writers get from individual editors varies enormously depending on their personalities. Some have a reputation for being exceptionally kind and supportive, others less so, but they all have one thing in common. Despite appearances to the contrary, they would all genuinely like to be able to publish your work.

If, therefore, they take the trouble to send you their editorial guidelines, study them carefully to ensure that the manuscripts you submit fit the brief you have been given as closely as possible.

Reading the magazine

There is no doubt that nothing irritates an editor more than receiving manuscripts from writers who have clearly never read their magazine. Almost all editorial guidelines urge would-be contributors to read the publication over a lengthy period before submitting any manuscripts. As stated above, magazines revamp on a regular basis, so you really need to study the format over several months.

Duplicating ideas

Reading the stories each week not only gives you an idea of the type of characters, themes and settings you should feature, but also stops you duplicating storylines. One of the commonest reasons for rejection is that your story is just too similar to one already accepted for publication.

Bridget Davidson, fiction editor of *Yours*, a magazine aimed primarily at the mature reader, lists the following themes to avoid:

◆ death
◆ illness

- widowhood
- memory flashbacks
- old people going into old people's homes
- old people mourning the death of their spouses and then finding a new love at a tea dance/bowls club/library/old people's home.

Giving you a hint
Editors are always on the lookout for regular contributors. When they receive a manuscript for publication, they can tell very quickly whether the author is likely to repeat their success or whether this story is a one-off lucky fluke.

Once published in a particular magazine, you stand a better chance of having more accepted by the same editor. By the time you have had several stories published, you should have built up a rapport between you and it is at this stage in your relationship that you may be asked to produce something new.

Now is the time to seize the opportunity to ask them exactly what they are looking for in the fiction you send them. Whilst the answers you receive may not be as enlightening as you had hoped, you will at least gain an insight into what you are up against. When you tentatively suggest a storyline, the response will probably be something along the following lines:

- 'Not sure, send me a draft and I'll cast an eye over it.'
- 'I've never tried that before, write it up and see how it turns out.'
- 'Sounds OK, let me have a look at it sometime.'

- 'I'm not sure what I want exactly, but I'll know it when I see it.'

That last statement is my favourite and the editor who made it will almost certainly recognise herself, as will her regular contributors.

Similar responses will also be given when you are past the awful stage of receiving standard rejection slips and as a reward for your patient perseverance in the face of adversity, are offered a crumb of explanation when your manuscript is returned.

Editors work under enormous pressure and it really isn't possible for them to give every contributor a blow-by-blow résumé of why their manuscript was unsuitable. The best you can hope for, apart from, 'this would be fine if you could just cut out all the characters and change the beginning, middle and end,' is something along the following lines:

- 'I'm afraid this isn't suitable for our magazine.'
- 'This doesn't quite work.'
- 'We no longer take stories on this theme.'
- 'This is too sharp/soft/complicated/slow/fast...etc. for our readers.'

(For submission guidelines from the fiction editors themselves, see Figures 13 and 14 on pages 196–7 and 199.)

It is an accepted truth among fiction writers that the stories you are sure are absolutely perfect for a particular magazine will invariably be rejected whilst the ones you are a little nervous about are, more often than not, accepted.

It is, therefore, best to write about characters and themes that interest you for magazines you enjoy reading. By having fun with your writing and producing stories for readers with whom you have an empathy, you will not only increase your own personal satisfaction but also your chances of having your stories accepted for publication.

CASE STUDIES

Elizabeth writes a romance
Elizabeth is an English graduate in her early thirties. She never reads women's magazines but is sure that the stories must be very simple to write. Having made the assumption that the sort of person who enjoys reading magazine fiction will be looking for escapism, she writes a 10,000 word story about a young heiress to a country estate, who falls in love with the stable lad. She sends it to *Woman* magazine because she remembers her mother reading it some twenty years ago. It is returned with a standard rejection slip.

Carol faces reality
Although Carol's children are still in their early teens, they are both planning to go away to college. Concerned about how she will cope when they have gone, she writes a story about the emotions a mother experiences when her last child leaves home and she finds herself alone with her husband for the first time in over twenty years. The story,

told from the heart, offers an identifiable situation for the readership of several women's magazines.

CHECKLIST

1. Are your stories too long for the popular fiction market?

2. Are you writing purely for a specialist genre?

3. Do you enjoy reading women's magazine fiction?

4. Can you genuinely relate to the readership of the magazines you have selected?

5. Do you enjoy writing fictional stories?

ASSIGNMENT

Select a magazine you enjoy and which considers unsolicited fiction and write down four themes you feel would appeal to the readership. Choose the one you feel most comfortable with and draft out a storyline, making sure that your characters fall into the right age group and reflect the right attitudes. Now write the story, keeping as close as possible to the length, style and format of your chosen story slot.

Are your stories too long for the popular fiction market?

7

Caring For Your Characters

IDENTIFYING WITH YOUR CHARACTERS

Being the man in a woman's world

It is a common misconception among male writers that by using a female pseudonym when re-submitting a previously rejected manuscript, an unsuitable story will magically become acceptable to women's magazine editors.

Nothing could be further from the truth. A surprising number of men write very successfully for the women's market and a masculine name is neither a help nor a hindrance to having work accepted for publication.

Whilst many male writers achieve most success with twist-end stories, there is also a healthy sprinkling producing fiction for lifestyle and romance slots. Contrary to common belief, it is not necessary to be female to relate either to the readership or to the problems that beset their daily lives.

For example, the following topics are equally relevant to both sexes and are ideal themes for magazine short stories:

- attending a much-needed job interview
- bringing up a child single-handed

+ facing life after being widowed/divorced
+ falling in love
+ finding yourself deep in debt
+ imminent parenthood
+ supermarket shopping
+ the pressures of unemployment on a relationship
+ unfair treatment at work.

Seeing life through the eyes of your characters
Characters in magazine fiction must:

+ reflect the age and social status of your readership
+ be people to whom your readers can relate
+ do the same sort of jobs as your readers
+ live in the same sort of areas and homes as your readers
+ have the same dreams, hopes and fears as your readers
+ use the same vocabulary as your readers.

A good short story is one which takes a little bit of daily life and gives the reader a smattering of hope. It allows the reader to believe that love can overcome any obstacle, that good does triumph over evil and that it is possible to win through against all the odds.

Liking the people you portray
Liking your characters is perhaps the most important aspect of fiction writing. If you don't care whether or not they achieve their aims, then nor will the reader.

Even if the villains are nasty through and through, you have to care what happens to them. They must have a vulnerable spot to which the reader can relate. This should not excuse their actions but should give them a realistic reason for going off the rails.

Sympathising with the heroine

Your heroine must be attractive without being too glamorous. She should look good enough for the readers to like her and sympathise with her plight but not so beautiful that she could never possibly be mistaken for one of them.

Her problems will be instantly recognisable to the readership as the following examples demonstrate:

◆ not wanting to be hurt by a partner again
◆ choosing between love and a career
◆ feeling under pressure to have a baby
◆ suspecting her partner is having an affair
◆ rebuilding a relationship after splitting up.

Relating to the viewpoint character

The viewpoint character is the one whose story you are telling either in the:

◆ first person viewpoint, i.e. 'I never thought this would happen to me.'

or in the

◆ third person viewpoint, i.e. 'She never thought this would happen to her.'

The advantage of using first person viewpoint is that the writer can assume the role of the central character and so relate to them completely.

With third person, you are removed from the protagonist and there is a danger that you will switch from one character to another, making the story confusing and losing all reader identification.

However, whilst first person may appear to be the best option, it can be a very limiting style and some fiction editors prefer the more flexible third person viewpoint in the stories they publish.

Avoiding viewpoint switches

One way to avoid switching viewpoint is to remember that the viewpoint character is the only one whose thoughts are known to you. For example:

> Karen glanced nervously from one to the other. She knew she was right for the job but would they agree?
>
> 'Congratulations, Miss Carson.' At the warmth of his smile, Karen felt the tension flow from her body. 'We'll be happy to take you on.' He lifted an enquiring eyebrow, 'When will you be free to start work?'

Although the interviewer is speaking, we are seeing the scene entirely through Karen's thoughts and emotions, making her the viewpoint character.

SIMPLIFYING THE PLOT

Because magazine fiction is designed to be a kind of 'quick fix' read, plots tend to be rather one-dimensional.

Every story must have conflict between the characters, in the form of differences of opinion between them or obstacles they have to overcome. In fiction, conflict does not necessarily mean that your characters are constantly fighting with one another. It is simply a device by which you introduce problems for your characters to solve, either between them or together as a couple.

Changing the lives of your characters

In very short stories, 500–1,500 words, the story is simply an incident in a character's life. However, no matter how small the incident, it should leave you in no doubt that the character's life will have been irrevocably changed.

In a longer story, you may have room for perhaps one minor sub-plot, but nothing too complicated or you will be unable to do it justice within the confines of a short story format.

Keeping it simple

Take, for example, a storyline about a young, newly-married couple moving into an old family house. The conflict could be that they bought the house with the idea of starting a family but having scraped together the purchase price, there is now no way they can afford to have a child.

This will provide your central theme, but to give it more substance, perhaps there is a history to the house. It's not a terribly grand property but they discover that it had belonged to one family for several generations. There is, your heroine feels, a wonderful homely atmosphere about the place. Looking up from the narrow hallway, she can visualise how it must have been, crammed full of happy, laughing children.

She decides to investigate the history of the original owners, offering a sub-plot in the form of the problems her predecessors encountered when setting up their home together. She discovers that they both began life in service but through hard work, managed to better themselves until they were in a position to marry and rent the old house. Not until their children had grown and were contributing to the family income, were they able to buy the house and achieve security for their old age.

The original theme about the newlyweds' dilemma will be kept to the forefront of the story, but comparison with the past will enable the heroine to choose her course of action.

Making the right choices

Her decision will be heavily influenced by the type of person she is and the readership of the magazine.

For a magazine aimed at independent career women, the sub-plot may serve as a warning to think about your motives before making the decision to have a baby. Looking at how tough life was for the children of impoverished parents in the past, the heroine may feel it is better to wait until she can afford to leave work and devote her time totally to her baby.

For a magazine that requires a more romantic outlook, the heroine will decide that it is not possible to put a price on happiness. She may not be able to give her child material things but judging by the previous occupants of her house, all you really need for your baby to thrive is love.

SETTINGS AND BACKGROUNDS

For your readers to relate to the characters in your stories, the settings and backgrounds must be instantly recognisable.

Apart from an historical romance, it is unlikely that having your heroine living a privileged lifestyle in luxurious surroundings will cut much ice with the average women's magazine reader. Characters in magazine fiction tend to inhabit the following dwellings:

◆ council houses
◆ flats in high-rise blocks, converted houses or above shops
◆ 3-4 bedroomed semis
◆ bedsits.

Very occasionally, they live in old folks' homes or thatched country cottages but these are the exception rather than the rule.

Geographically, magazine fiction characters may live anywhere from John O'Groats to Lands End, in a rural community or on an inner-city housing estate. The only rule is that the reader must be able to identify with them.

LISTENING IN ON CONVERSATIONS

Listening in on conversations.

Magazine stories contain a high proportion of dialogue and there are two main reasons for this:

1. Dialogue = Pace, i.e. keeps the story moving, and you must have a fast pace if you are to successfully fill the small slot allocated to you.

2. People love eavesdropping on other people's conversations.

Describing the characters

One of the most effective methods of letting your readers know what is happening in a story is through the conversations your characters have with one another. Good dialogue should:

◆ describe the characters' appearance
◆ explain what has gone before
◆ give a hint of what is about to come
◆ move the story forward
◆ offer a clear insight into the characters' personalities.

We'll be looking at how you show the reader what is happening through a combination of dialogue and action in Chapter 12. It should be possible, however, to tell who is speaking to whom simply from the vocabulary used, without any description at all.

Speaking naturally

Study the sentences below and see if you can tell who the characters are (answers on page 225). It should be quite clear not only who is speaking but also the person they are talking to:

1. 'Look, here's your mummy in this photo. You look just like her when she was your age.'

2. 'You won't regret this. I've been dying to have a go at your hair colour. I promise you won't recognise yourself. It'll take years off you.'

3. 'I'm pleased to tell you that the X-rays were clear. You've had a lucky escape this time but if you don't ease back on your workload and cut down on your smoking and drinking, you won't get away with it again.'

Standing on the dialogue alone

For short passages, good dialogue will stand on its own without the need for any action or description at all. For example:

'Here, Linda, try this lipstick.. I'd buy it like a shot if I had fair hair like you. The colour'll look great against your pale skin.

> 'D'you think so? I'm not sure. It looks a bit bright to me.
> I usually prefer reddish-browns to shocking pinks.'

It's quite obvious that the two characters are women friends out shopping and from their conversation, we know a little about them. We know that:

* Linda has fair hair and pale skin
* from her choice of lipstick, she's quite conservative in her appearance
* that her friend is much more lively and adventurous
* that her friend has a darker complexion and hair.

We also know which one is speaking and exactly what they are doing. Any description or action would be superfluous.

We can, however, change the characterisation by making a few alterations to the dialogue, still without using any description:

> 'Excuse me Madam, would you like to try this lipstick? I must say, I wouldn't hesitate to buy it if I had fair hair like you. The colour will set off your pale complexion beautifully.

> 'D'you think so? It looks a bit bright to me. I usually prefer reddish-browns to shocking pinks. Still, I suppose it's worth giving it a go.'

The conversation is intrinsically the same but by adding a few words and changing others, we have two entirely new characters, in the form of a sales girl on a cosmetic counter and an easy-going customer.

SOLVING PROBLEMS

As mentioned above, conflict is vital to any work of fiction. In every story that you write, you must give your central character a problem to solve.

Empowering your characters

Having created characters you care about, it can be tempting to try to sort out all their problems for them. An understandable emotion, but one which must be firmly squashed if you are to write effectively for the magazine market.

Many of your readers will identify with the problems in your stories and, although they won't expect solutions to be handed to them on a plate, will be looking for a note of hope in the stories you write.

The following solutions are just a few you should avoid at all costs:

- Timely intervention by a well-meaning elderly person, i.e. the wise old lady or gentleman who helps your character see the error of their ways.

- A useful coincidence, i.e. the guy chatting up your heroine reveals he is a plumber, car mechanic, plasterer or whatever who can fix her leak, engine or hole in her wall.

- A lottery win just in time to save the character from financial ruin.

- The boyfriend conveniently deciding to move out just as your heroine was going to break off their relationship.

Working it out for themselves

Waving a metaphorical magic wand over the situation to waft all the problems away is a hopeless cheat. The reader wants to see how the characters cope and move on with their lives, so let them work it out for themselves. Put yourself in their place. What would you do if:

- Your car broke down?
- Your central heating packed up?
- You felt the need to confront your partner about your relationship?

OK, maybe in real life you would call the AA, pick a plumber at random from *Yellow Pages* or squash any nagging doubts and just get on with your life but that's not the stuff good fiction is made of.

You need to have your characters interacting with one another, so go back and think what your central character would do.

Setting up the situation

Is she the capable type who can strip a car down and reassemble it without having six washers and a length of rubber hose left over? If so, when her car breaks down, she'll fix it herself. To make a story out of that situation, you'll either have to set her somewhere isolated and scary or have her falling for a 'new' man who'll cook, clean and be prepared to be a stay-at-home dad when the first baby arrives.

Seeking a manly shoulder

Today's heroines are unlikely to admit to actively seeking a man who will whisk them off to a life of domestic bliss. They may reluctantly be forced to confess to needing a man to perform traditionally masculine tasks, but this will add to the conflict between them. On the whole, your female characters should be relatively self-sufficient.

Switching roles

Male characters can be anything from caring single parents to male chauvinist pigs. They can be very sensitive and understanding about the problems their girlfriends and wives face. Alternatively, they could be total slobs, depending on the tone and style of the story and the magazine at which it is aimed.

Heroes can be just as concerned about developments in their relationships as their female counterparts and may be facing up to the problems associated with competition in the workplace, retirement, widowhood and getting on with the neighbours in just the same way.

RAISING HOPES

Writers should aim for uplifting endings for their stories which may not necessarily be happy but will give the reader hope.

For example, a story aimed at a magazine for over-forties might have a widow new to the area as its central character. She and her husband retired to their dream bungalow but shortly after they arrived he died, leaving her alone in a strange town.

This situation is all too common and sadly one to which many older readers will relate. If the widow is portrayed as being unable to cope, it would be far too painful for many readers to handle. As a writer, you have a responsibility to your readers to find a way for her to come to terms with what has happened and move on with her life.

Offering a way through

There are no instant solutions to this problem and your readers are well aware of that. There may, however, be a way through for them by offering them some options. Your central character could:

- sell up and move back to her old neighbourhood
- embark on a fund-raising project in memory of her husband
- take the first step to rebuilding a social life by inviting a neighbour to lunch
- volunteer to help with a planned community event
- book a trip to somewhere she has always wanted to go.

If the route you choose for your character offers just one reader a choice they hadn't previously considered, then it will be a huge achievement in your fiction writing career.

CASE STUDIES

George tries his hand at murder

George is a crime fiction devotee in his late forties. He has successfully written some stories for a small press crime magazine he subscribes to and decides to try his hand at his wife's weekly women's magazine. The story, which he submits under the pen name Georgiana Flintlock, is about a henpecked wimp who is killed by his wife because he forgets to take her a cup of tea in bed before he leaves for work in the morning. The lack of a realistic motive for murder combined with George's concern about revealing his true identity to his intended readership ensures a swift rejection.

Rob switches roles

Rob is a computer programmer in his late twenties. His story, aimed at a women's magazine for the under forties' market, has the reader following the protagonist through every stage of advanced pregnancy from food cravings, relaxation and breathing exercises, misgivings about the decision to have a baby and labour pains to the emotional high of giving birth, until the twist end reveals that the central 'I' character is, in fact, the baby's father. The story is accepted and published under Rob's own name.

CHECKLIST

1. Do you care what happens to your characters?

2. Will magazine readers relate to the characters and situations in your story?

3. Will your story fit into a specific magazine 'slot'?

4. Is the dialogue in your story realistic?

5. Will your readership relate to the vocabulary you use?

ASSIGNMENT

Magazine short stories reflect everyday situations. Write a confrontational conversation between a couple under stress packing to go on holiday. As the dialogue between them develops, see if you can expand the scene into a short story.

8

Finding the Right Format

ROMANCING THE READER

As mentioned in previous chapters, the market for romantic fiction has shrunk over the past few years.

Waiting for Mr Right

Whilst characters in magazine fiction still fall in love and even get married, the whole concept of 'waiting for Mr Right' to come along and sweep the heroine off her feet is no longer an acceptable theme.

Today's romantic fiction is all about making choices. The central character will have to decide her course of action from a number of options:

- ◆ Does she commit herself to marriage or retain her independence by staying single?

- ◆ Does she give up her career to follow her man or must he give up his to follow her?

- ◆ Is a good sex life the basis on which to commit herself to a long-term relationship?

- ◆ Is she prepared to work on a relationship with the children of the man she loves?

- ◆ Having divorced her husband, should she now give him another chance?

- Can she risk falling in love again after being badly hurt before?

Laughing at love

All the themes listed above overlap between the categories of romance and lifestyle.

However, there is still room for some old-fashioned romance, where the girl is out to trap her man, but these usually have more than a hint of humour about them. They tend to be either:

- quirky tales where the central character appears to be disinterested in her quarry but tricks him into asking her out

or

- typically triangular tales, where the heroine is involved with one rather unsavoury character, whilst another much more acceptable but less exciting prospect waits patiently in the wings.

With the second type of story, the humour generally comes in the form of romantic banter between the hopeful lover and the heroine. Comparing it with the serious, often demanding relationship she has with her boyfriend, realisation slowly dawns on the central character that the couple that laughs together, stays together.

Making love

Love scenes can be quite explicit in some magazines. Some of the titles aimed at the under-forties are prepared to include stories with an erotic flavour, although as with all romantic fiction, the emphasis should always be on love, rather than sex.

For *Bella's* 2,000-word romances, fiction editor Linda O'Byrne's guidelines state that the story should have:

> 'A central love interest, plenty of conflict, warmth, emotion and an understanding that physical sex exists between people in love! There should be a happy or hopeful ending. Not usually a traditional boy-meets-girl story but rather the problems encountered in an established relationship. The main characters should both play a part in resolving their difficulties.'

LOOKING AT LIFESTYLES

For many of today's magazines, the emphasis for their short story characters is on lifestyle rather than romance.

Living the lives of your readers

These stories reflect the lives of the readership and like their romantic counterparts, offer choices, rather than solutions. Lifestyle topics include:

- examining attitudes to in-laws
- handling sensitive situations in the workplace
- becoming an 'empty-nester', i.e. seeing your children grow up and leave home
- inviting ex-spouses and their partners to weddings
- adopted children tracking down their natural parents
- meeting the child you gave up for adoption
- setting up home with a step-family
- rebuilding your life after a tragedy.

In other words, anything at all that your readership might experience in their own lives. Providing it is handled sensitively, almost any topic can be covered, but every story must end on a note of hope.

Reflecting reality

Any one of the above situations could form the basis of a magazine lifestyle story. In order to give it maximum reader appeal, you have to be sure that the sentiments you are portraying not only reflect those of your intended readership but also of you, the writer.

For example, the 'empty-nester' storyline offers an apparently ideal scenario for a magazine aimed at the over-fifties. A charming image of loving Mum and Dad mourning the departure of their newly independent offspring from their well-appointed family home.

Perhaps Mum could take a positive stance, viewing the changes as an opportunity to spread her own wings and distance herself from domesticity by returning to education or the job she once enjoyed. Never mind about Dad, his function could be to provide the conflict by having to be supported in accepting the changes happening around him.

Finding common ground

For some markets, however, these attitudes simply won't do. The cosy, middle-class lifestyle portrayed above offers choices that, depending on the target audience, many of your intended readers may not have.

There is also the overriding factor, common at this stage of so many relationships, that one or both of the partners may consider the children to be the only cement holding them together as a couple at all.

Their home may be cramped and uncomfortable. Not a home at all in the true sense of the word but simply the place they return to after a hard day's work. Either or both partners may have been forced to work in jobs they hated in order to make ends meet and support their offspring. Now, with the children off their hands, they are free to consider options that may never have been possible before. Of course, they could decide to stay together and make the best of a bad job, but for our purposes, this would only work if it could be shown that this solution offered the promise of better things to come. More attractive possibilities might be to:

◆ Split up, sell up and move on to better things.

◆ Talk it through and agree on changes that offer them the promise of happier life together.

◆ Talk it through and discover there is more than enough common ground on which to rebuild the love for one another they believed they had lost.

SELECTING THE VIEWPOINT CHARACTER

In order to gain the maximum impact in a short story, it is essential that you choose your viewpoint, or central, character with care.

This involves choosing a character with whom the readers can instantly identify and for many of today's women's magazines, this character will be female. Ideally, she should have a strong personality but she should certainly not be aggressive or unpleasant. Not if the readers are to care about the decisions she makes.

If she takes the first option, splitting up and moving on, it should be because this will be her last chance to make a new life for herself. Providing her with a rich lover to whisk her off to a life of luxury as soon as she's dumped the poor guy she's led a dog's life for the past 20 years is unlikely to endear her to her target audience.

Perhaps surprisingly, however, talking it through and sorting out her differences with her partner may not offer the preferred solution if there is a chance it could be viewed as an unsatisfactory compromise by the reader. She has to be sure that the character with whom she so strongly identifies is getting the very best out of any deal she is persuaded to strike.

Making men happy

Fortunately, women's magazines are prepared to consider the possibility that men have feelings too. Although a growing number prefer the viewpoint character to be female, some are still prepared to consider a male protagonist, provided he complies with a few basic standards of behaviour.

For example, your male central character is invariably strong but sensitive. He will be fully aware that there are issues that need addressing between himself and his partner and must be prepared to compromise in order to sort them out.

The splitting up and moving on scenario is not going to be an option for him. The readers are unlikely to let him get away with that. His best hope is to show them how vulnerable he is feeling and that he is prepared to make the changes necessary to forge a better life together. It will also help his cause if he is prepared to give his partner total support in any new ventures she may be planning.

GOING BACK IN TIME
The market for historical stories is another area that has shrunk. Perhaps the best opportunities in this field are to be found in magazines specialising in romantic fiction.

Picturing the scene
In order to write effective historical fiction, both you and the reader must be able to picture the scene you are setting. The following points are essential:

- in-depth knowledge of the period in which your story is set
- vocabulary which reflects the manner of speech of the period
- accuracy with regard to costumes and hairstyles
- a knowledge of the modes of transport and journey times
- accurate knowledge of the food consumed and how it would be prepared
- in-depth understanding of the etiquette of the period.

DEVISING SERIALS
Because of the detail required in order to convey an historical background effectively, these tend to be featured as serials, rather than one-off short stories.

Markets for serials are very limited but one major title still prepared to take them is *Woman's Weekly*. Fiction editor Gaynor Davies offers the following tips for new writers in her helpful and comprehensive writers' guidelines:

> Serials should have all the compelling qualities of short stories – strong characterisation and a well-researched background – and must also have riveting cliffhangers to keep the reader going back to the newsagent week after week! There should be a central 'hook' to hang the action on; an emotional or practical dilemma which the heroine has to face. A strong subplot and well-researched background are essential. Historicals are just as welcome as contemporary serials.
>
> Serials can be between 2 and 5 parts. The opening instalment is 4,500 words and each subsequent instalment is 3,500 words.
>
> You may submit the whole of your manuscript, or just the first part with a brief synopsis. A synopsis alone cannot be considered; we need to be able to assess your style too.'

CASE STUDIES

Philippa falls in love

Philippa is a mature, well-educated lady, keen to write contemporary romances for the women's magazine market. Her exquisitely beautiful heroines, with their perfect diction and wealthy backgrounds lack only one thing, a strong, handsome man to love and care for them. Unfortunately, the combination of stilted dialogue, unrealistic settings and a lack of understanding about contemporary lifestyle issues results in repeated rejections.

Karen remarries

It was whilst she was writing her wedding guest list that divorcee Karen had to decide whether or not to invite her ex-husband. As she pondered over the implications of inviting ex-spouses to second weddings, she realised that a large proportion of her target readership probably shared her problem. With names changed and a few fictional embellishments to achieve the desired result, her completed short story was accepted for publication.

CHECKLIST

1. Are the themes of your stories relevant to today's magazine readers?

2. Could your story be expanded to serial length?

3. Is any historical content accurate?

4. Are there situations in your own life that your target readership could relate to?

5. Are you aiming your story at the right market?

ASSIGNMENT

Read the following passage, then answer the questions to help you decide whether the story should be a romance or lifestyle:

> A married couple have just moved into the neighbourhood. It is Saturday morning and the husband has stayed at home to look after their six-month-old baby whilst the wife has gone shopping. She returns with a friend, a girl she was a school with who, it turns out, lives just round the corner. The minute he sets eyes on the friend, the husband's jaw drops and he goes quite pale.*

Note: If you prefer, you can turn the situation round, so that the husband brings a male friend home and it is the wife who reacts.

1. How old are the characters?

2. What are their names?

3. What do they look like?

4. Do they have jobs and if so, what do they do?

5. What is the cause of the spouse's reaction?

6. How will he deal with the situation?

7. Which character do you relate to most strongly?

8. What happens next?

Are you aiming your story at the right market?

9

Creating a Twist in the Tale

DEFINING THE TWIST IN THE TALE

One short story format we have not yet explored is the twist or sting in the tale. At the time of writing, so many women's magazines publish twist stories, that novice writers can be misled into believing that all magazine short stories must have a twist ending.

In fact, for some magazines, the reverse is true and they will not even consider manuscripts with any kind of surprise ending. It is important, therefore, to understand how the construction of a twist story differs from other short story formats.

Twisting the tale

A good twist in the tale is not unlike a magician's illusion. Working on the principle that seeing is believing, the illusionist makes use of the fact that the eye can be very deceptive. By keeping the audience transfixed on the events onstage, the mechanics of the illusion are concealed from view in such a way that only a trained onlooker will be able to detect how the trick is done.

Using diversionary tactics

The most effective illusionists are those who build up the tension through a combination of theatrical costume, clever lighting and dramatic sets. Common sense tells us that it's just a trick. However, the scene being played out onstage transfixes the audience into believing that the impossible is happening before their eyes.

Using the same concept, albeit in a less dramatic form, the main theme in a twist story is an illusion. Something else is always going on behind the scenes.

Deceiving the reader

There are two main types of twist stories:

1. Those in which the central character appears to be getting away with something but is effectively hoist with his or her own petard at the end.

2. Those in which the characters are not who or what they appear to be.

The twist author sets out to deceive the reader and achieves this by a combination of strong characterisation, subtle double-edged clues and a somewhat quirky attitude of mind.

Setting up the signposts

One of the commonest misconceptions about twist-end stories is that the key is in concealing the truth from the reader. In fact, in order to achieve the desired result, it is essential that you keep the reader fully informed by sprinkling subtle 'signposts' or clues throughout the story. For example, in the following extract from a story entitled 'Act Your Age!' who do you think the characters are?

Mandy eyed her mother's back impatiently, 'For heavens' sake,' she muttered, dropping her bag noisily on the kitchen floor. 'Mum! Hurry up! I'll be late for school at this rate.'

Hopefully, you have correctly identified them as mother and daughter, but what about Mandy's age? If you've assumed she is a teenager, then that is just the result I was aiming for.

However, things are never what they seem in a twist story, so it helps to consider possible alternatives. As the story progresses, it becomes clear that Mandy is becoming increasingly unhappy about her divorced mother's relationship with their recently widowed next door neighbour:

'Mum, you're not going out tonight are you?' she frowned at the large gold earrings slapping at her mother's jaw, wishing she could turn the clock back to the days when it was just the two of them and she behaved and dressed like a real mum.

Mandy had even teased her once that, with her neat perm and her frilly apron, she looked exactly like the mother in those old first reading books – where the children played ball with the dog and father wore sleeveless pullovers.

Adèle Ramet, *Bella Summer Special* 1997

By now, you should be getting a bit suspicious because, if you think about it, mothers haven't dressed this way for at least 40 years. In fact, by the end of the story, it is revealed that far from being a teenager, Mandy is a schoolteacher, well into her thirties. Whilst her mother is, perhaps, a little long in the tooth for her new T-shirt and jeans image, having devoted her life to single-handedly raising a daughter, she has every intention of grabbing what she perceives to be her last chance of happiness.

Cheating never works

At no time was the reader ever cheated in this story. Although the initial impression is of a sulky teenager, it is the phrase, 'late for school', that immediately plants the misleading image in the reader's mind. However, the phrase could just as easily be uttered by a teacher as a pupil.

As with all other forms of magazine fiction, situations and settings must be instantly recognisable and the twist writer capitalises on this by gently nudging the reader towards forming the wrong conclusion.

BEGINNING WITH THE ENDING

One of the commonest mistakes novice writers make when they attempt to write fiction is to begin writing aimlessly, with no idea where the storyline is going to take them. This approach may sound wonderfully artistic and creative, but it invariably results in a rambling tale, full of stops, starts and viewpoint changes.

Writing backwards

The most effective way to approach a twist in the tale is to think of an ending, then work out how you are going to achieve it. To all intents and purposes, therefore, the skilled twist author writes backwards.

Creating identifiable characters

The skill of the short story writer lies in developing identifiable characters who interact realistically with one another and their surroundings. Under these circumstances, the author can effectively interpret the interplay, provide suitably atmospheric settings and oversee events to their logical conclusion.

Changing the outcome

This is not to say that the storyline cannot change. In a straightforward three-handed romance, for example, the reader will expect the girl to choose the right boy from two very different suitors. The writer's initial intention may be for her to choose the solid reliable one, but as the story progresses in its non-twist format, the circumstances could alter, as illustrated in the sample three-handed romance format in Figure 7.

Possible outcomes depending on Jill's character

1. Jill decides to stay with Bob. He will always be there for her and whilst Matt's lifestyle sounds exciting, she could never be sure of his commitment to her.

2. Jill runs off with Matt. She cannot stay with Bob if he is going to make major decisions like where they will live without consulting her.

The choice Jill makes will depend on how her personality evolves as the story progresses, but a twist tale has a far more complicated structure.

There is no leeway in a twist story to allow the characters to take off in a direction of their own. We need to know right at the start who will end up with whom and why.

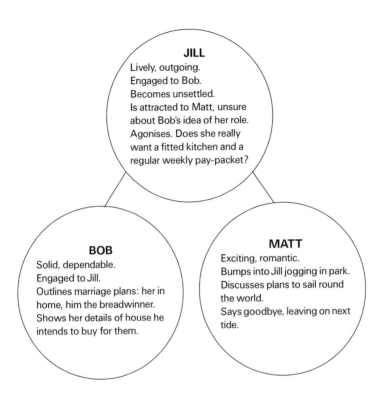

Fig. 7. Sample three-handed romance format.

Constructing a twist

In the twisted version of our three-handed romance, the writer might be working towards an ending in which Jill is left high and dry while the two men sail off happily together into the sunset.

Once we know the outcome, we can direct our characters to set the traps and then spring them for us in all the right places. We will be looking at methods of setting those traps, or 'signposting', later in the book. First, we must think about the storyline and then ask ourselves that vital question, 'What if...?'

TWISTING THE 'WHAT IF?' FACTOR

Ask any writer how they come up with their plots and they will probably tell you that they think of either a character or a situation and then ask themselves the question 'what if...?'

The same technique is true of the twist in the tale but for our purposes, the 'what if?' factor must have a slight kink in it.

Sample twist storyline

A young woman is waiting for her long-term boyfriend in the lobby of a large office block. *What if* he fails to turn up? There are a number of options:

- ◆ He's stood her up.
- ◆ He's had an accident.
- ◆ He forgot that he would be working late.

Any one of these examples would work as a romantic story but the twist writer will be looking for an angle and this is where you will find a somewhat cynical or twisted outlook is invaluable.

The cynical approach

Sifting though the above options, I find myself most attracted to the second one, where the poor chap has a, possibly fatal, accident.

The heroine has been waiting for some time. Her colleagues are leaving and soon the steady stream of office workers thins to a trickle. A security guard notices her anxiously consulting her watch. He strikes up a conversation with her and she tells him all about her relationship. She hints that her boyfriend can be quite cruel, but in spite of his shortcomings, she loves him. He's very late and she's sure something must have happened to him. They discuss the possibility that she might have been mistaken about the time and place but she assures him that her boyfriend confirmed the arrangements by phone only a few hours before.

The girl becomes more distraught until, in an effort to set her mind at rest, the security guard offers to telephone first their apartment and then her boyfriend's office. You may need to come up with a reason why she is unable to use a mobile phone. Perhaps her battery is flat or the signal too weak. With no reply from either home or the office, the security guard discreetly telephones the local hospital. Yes, he is told, there has been a fatal accident.

It is at this point that the cynical twist writer reveals the true question, which is not, 'what if he fails to turn up?' but 'what if the heroine knew he wasn't going to turn up all along?'.

Setting the trap

She has, of course, set up the accident and the wait in the office lobby is her alibi. The security guard will confirm her distressed state. Fellow employees from the insurance company where she works saw her waiting and when she collects on the policy she recently took out on her boyfriend's life, her colleagues will believe that she has something to cushion the blow of her loss.

PLOTTING AND PLANNING

Twist stories can be quite complex but this does not mean that they are heavily plotted. The small number of words counts against the twist writer.

Keeping it simple

With a limited number of characters, a limited timescale and, in some cases, as few as 500 words, any attempt to work out a complicated plotline, full of red herrings and suspicious characters, is going to end in awful failure. In the case of a magazine twist in the tale story, the intricacies of the plot must be dealt with as briefly as possible.

However, provided you avoid deviating too far from the basic plotline, it is possible to introduce a note of flexibility. For example, the basic plot for our young lady and her accident-prone boyfriend was relatively simple, but *what if* it turns out to be a case of mistaken identity and it wasn't him who was killed at all? Or perhaps he was killed but not in the way our heroine planned and she is unable to collect on the policy.

You may come up with a number of variations but the basic plotline must not change, i.e. *A girl is waiting for a man who she knows is not going to arrive.*

As the characters begin to develop, so you can plan the course of events. It is at this stage that you will be able to make your decision about the final twist, but be sure you have it firmly fixed in your mind before you attempt to finish the story.

FRAMING THE VICTIM

The central character in a twist story may well be the perpetrator of a particularly unpleasant crime. One of the problems a twist writer has to solve, therefore, is how to let the protagonist commit the crime and get away with it without upsetting the reader's moral sensibilities.

Sympathising with the murderer

In the plot outlined above, our heroine hinted to the security guard that her boyfriend had a cruel streak. Maybe he thinks nothing of giving her a good beating, plays around with other women or is obsessively jealous. By the time we've finished with him, the reader will be as desperate as our heroine is to get rid of him and get their own back on him for his appalling behaviour.

Rebounding on the murderer

However, in this particular story, our central character could turn out to be the victim of her own vicious scheme. This time, the hatchet job must be applied to her character. Maybe she is lying about her boyfriend. He's weak and was easily tricked into making her the beneficiary of his insurance policy. When she is unable to collect on it, we are relieved that she hasn't got away with her plan.

MISLEADING ISN'T CHEATING

The art of twist story writing is to give the reader as much information as possible, but framed in such a way that nothing is exactly what it appears to be. This effect is achieved by the use of ambiguous words and phrases which are deliberately designed to mislead the reader.

Concealing the truth

The following extract is taken from a story I wrote entitled 'Face to Face'. The central characters are Toby and Jane, a married couple who appear to be interior decorators. The setting is a luxury flat they had hoped to purchase but couldn't afford. The couple have, apparently, been engaged by the new owners to advise on the renovations and décor:

> The sound of the front door crashing open broke into their conversation and Toby flew to the landing outside the flat.
>
> 'It's all right,' he reassured Jane as she reached his side, 'It's only the carpenter. He's stacking the new floorboards in the hall downstairs.' He let out a low, soft whistle, 'Just look at it all, I wouldn't like to have to lug that lot up these stairs.'
>
> 'You'd better watch out then,' Jane giggled, 'If he catches sight of you, he might try to rope you in to give him a hand.'
>
> (Adèle Ramet, *Bella* 1993)

It all sounds perfectly normal but there's something not quite right. Toby should be directing operations, not skulking about upstairs. In his line of work, he should know how many floorboards the carpenter will need.

Sprinkling clues

A couple of paragraphs on, Jane mentions how pleased she is that the new floor is going to be laid. '*That gaping hole,*' she says, '*really gives me the creeps.*' Toby, however, is quick to reassure her. '*It can't hurt you,*' he tells her. A truth which becomes clear when it is finally revealed that the couple are, in fact, ghosts, who met their death by crashing through rotten floorboards when they were viewing the property.

They fully intend to stay in their dream home, using their spiritual powers to influence the new owners into decorating the flat exactly the way they want it.

Revealing the truth

Far from concealing their true state, clues or 'signposts' have been liberally sprinkled throughout the story. The characters never actually touch anything, they '*work their way around the room*' and when they heard the carpenter arrive, Toby literally '*flew*' to the landing.

The story's final twist also explains why Jane '*giggled*' at the thought of the carpenter catching sight of Toby, a reaction that is glossed over when it happens but serves to reinforce the twist in the tale. It is the combination of dropped hints, subtle clues and equally subtle omissions that achieve reader satisfaction in a twist end story. Without them, the story has no substance and will be a disappointing cheat.

CASE STUDIES

Jill loses direction

Jill is a teacher in her early thirties, whose love of reading gives her the inspiration for unlimited original stories. Her opening lines are perfect, pulling you straight into the action and there is lots of vibrant dialogue between the characters, but halfway through, her stories lose impetus because she can never decide on the ending. She always hopes that, once she has begun to write, the characters will interact sufficiently with one another to indicate a suitable twist, but without a clear ending to aim for, Jill loses direction and is never able to construct a viable plot.

Barbara twists the tale

Barbara is a lively, enthusiastic single parent. Despite having been through some very difficult times, she has a well-developed, wry sense of humour, which she puts to excellent use in her twist stories. Her past experience has taught her that it can be very useful to expect the unexpected, so she is able to think up suitably devious endings as soon as her characters are formed in her mind. Only when she has decided on the ending does she work on the interaction between her characters to bring realism to the story.

CHECKLIST

1. Do you know how your story is going to end?

2. Is the 'what if?' question sufficiently twisted?

3. Is the plot too complicated?

4. Have you planned your story from start to finish?

5. Are you sure you have not cheated?

ASSIGNMENT

The following sentences are open to two different interpretations. I have set out the most obvious one, your task is to find the hidden meaning. (Answers are on page 225.)

Example: *Puffing and panting as he climbed higher and higher, he wondered if he would ever reach the top.*

(a) A man struggling up a mountain.
(b) A small child climbing a flight of stairs.

1. *The sea of faces waited expectantly for him to deliver his speech.*

    (a) A tutor delivering a lecture.

    (b) ....

2. *Deftly, she fastened off the row of neat stitches.*

    (a) A seamstress finishing off a garment.

    (b) ....

3. *She hated never being allowed to go anywhere by herself.*

    (a) A young girl.

    (b) ....

4. *Heads turned as he posed and strutted in time to the throbbing music.*

    (a) A John Travolta look-alike in a disco.

    (b) ....

(10)

Signposting

TAKING YOUR READER ALONG THE SCENIC ROUTE

As we saw in the previous chapter, in a twist story, it is essential that you do not cheat by concealing a vital piece of information and then revealing it at the end of the story. All this will do is to leave you with an unconvincing ending and a very disappointed reader.

Misdirecting the reader

In order to achieve an acceptable twist in the tale, you need to plant signposts which will effectively misdirect the reader along a number of side turnings before leading them finally to your intended destination. To help clarify this technique, think of writing straightforward romantic stories as travelling down a motorway, whilst twist stories take the scenic route.

With a romance, your route from beginning to end is mapped out but what, at first sight, appears to be a clear road, inevitably becomes strewn with obstacles. Traffic jams, diversions, unexpected incidents litter the highway but the couple steadfastly remain on the path to happiness, emerging relatively unscathed from their journey to spend the rest of their days firmly united.

Sidetracking

In a twist story, the writer deliberately avoids the motorway in favour of the country lanes. In this way, the reader becomes sidetracked by a variety of picturesque sights and sounds. We may potter along an old farmtrack or rest awhile at a riverside pub. The reader is never quite sure where we are going or even why we are going there, but whichever route we take, it is imperative that the sidetracks inevitably lead us back to where we ought to be.

PLANTING THE CLUES

We have looked briefly at some of the methods of using misleading signposts in the previous chapter; the technique of planting clues to convey information and move the story forward is found in all forms of short story writing. There are a number of ways you can do this:

- through dialogue
- through description
- through action
- through flashback.

Using dialogue

As we saw in Chapter 7, dialogue fulfils a number of functions in fiction and will reveal a great deal of useful information. In the story 'Face to Face', Jane is saddened by the fact that the couple who have purchased 'their' flat are unlikely to have children. She tells Toby:

> 'Somehow, I can't ever see children featuring in their lifestyle.'

'Definitely not. But then,' Toby's voice was gruff, 'things don't always work out the way we plan them, do they?'

At this stage in the story, we are still unaware that they are ghosts and this short piece of dialogue appears to refer to the fact that they were unable to buy the family home they wanted. With hindsight, however, we can see that it refers to their untimely death before they had a chance to start a family of their own.

Using description and action

The combination of description and action can be very effective in planting clues. From the following narrative, it would appear that E. Evans' story entitled 'Led Astray' (*Bella* 1995) is centred around a troublesome toddler:

> Josh closed his lips and turned his head away. He didn't want strained beef. He wanted chocolate pudding. He sensed she was in a hurry. Perhaps Chris was coming round. The thought of Chris made him pout. This gave her the chance to tip a spoonful of mush into his mouth. Spluttering, he spat it into his bib.

As the story progresses, it quickly becomes clear that all is far from well in this particular household. Through a fast-moving combination of dialogue, description and action, the reader is misled into believing that the story is about a young mother whose husband has been given an early release from a long prison sentence.

A conversation between the hated Chris and the woman, Sal, as she spoonfeeds Josh reveals a more worrying scenario:

Chris gripped her hands. 'We knew we had to face it sometime. Luke's got to know,' Josh caught the nod in his direction, 'You can't hide him, can you?' In fact, I'm surprised nobody's tipped Luke off.'

By now, the reader is thoroughly convinced. During Luke's time in prison, Sal and Chris have had an affair and baby Josh is the result.

Using flashback

It is at this point that E. Evans introduces flashback to heighten the tension further:

'Oh, Chris, I wish we'd gone away before he came back.'
'I wanted to. You're the one who wanted to stop here.'
'I couldn't let him come back to an empty house.'
'That's always been your trouble, Sal. You're too loyal. You should have got out years ago, instead of staying with a husband who knocked you about.'

Firmly hooked now, we read on to discover that Luke is a hardened criminal with a history of violence. In a vain attempt to delay the inevitable, Sal and Chris bundle Josh into his coat but just as they are wheeling him out of the kitchen, Luke arrives. They hurriedly push Josh into the lounge and shut the door but to no avail. Bored and irritable, Josh squeals and screams until he is discovered by the menacingly powerful Luke.

It is here that E. Evans once again uses flashback to reveal the very clever twist and bring the story to a highly satisfactory end. Josh is not, in fact, a toddler at all but Sal's husband and Luke's father. Shortly after 'shopping' his own son to the police, he was involved in a car accident which left him in this appallingly brain-damaged state. As if this were not enough, the author includes a final horrific twist as she reveals in the story's closing paragraph below that the car crash in which Josh received his injuries was no accident but had set up by an embittered, vengeful, Luke:

> Josh eyed the large man as he bent over him. He sensed he didn't like him.
>
> 'Well, well, Dad,' Luke murmured, 'Who'd have thought that brake would last for a whole year. I couldn't have frayed it enough when I was out on bail. Still, all's well that ends well, eh? That'll teach you to try to do me out of my cut from the post office job by setting me up with the police.'
>
> (E. Evans, *Bella* 1995)

TURNING AND TWISTING

A tale with a good single twist is very desirable and perfectly saleable. A double twist, one in which the reader is given two surprises, is even better, so it is worth taking a close look at your original storyline to see if it can be improved upon. However, most sought after of all is the triple twist which is not only the most difficult to write but also the most saleable format.

Twisting once, twice, three times

For the single twist, we know that we need the following elements:

- strong characterisation
- realistic dialogue

- action, reaction and interaction
- imaginative signposting
- originality.

Using the plot in the previous chapter about the young woman waiting for her boyfriend, the basic storyline offers only a single twist but by continuing to twist and turn, it is possible to introduce a double and even a triple twist, as shown in Figure 8.

Why not twist again?

In theory, there is no reason why a fourth twist could not be added to this storyline.

The confirmation of the boyfriend's death could be due to a case of mistaken identity on the part of the hospital. The story's final twist could then have the boyfriend returning home to discover his late girlfriend's body. A fitting end, if only there were enough room for it on the page.

Running out of words

It is a skilful writer indeed who can manage more than three twists within the confines of a one-page slot and still find room for characterisation and background information.

The discipline of writing stories for women's magazines is a strict one, offering little freedom to wander away from the initial plot. A fourth twist is near impossible to achieve effectively in 850–1,000 words.

Single Twist

1	2	3	4
Girl waits, apparently anxiously, for boyfriend.	She knows he will not arrive because she has arranged for him to meet with an accident.	Her plan succeeds, he dies.	Insurance company pays out.

Double Twist

1	2	3	4
Girl waits for boy.	She knows he will not arrive.	Her plan succeeds, he dies.	Query on insurance.
5	**6**	**7**	**8**
There is a hitch. He is dead but not from the cause she planned.	Suicide is suspected and payment will be withheld.	She cannot prove otherwise without implicating herself.	Her plan has failed. The tables are turned on her.

Triple Twist

1	2	3	4
Girl waits for boy.	She knows he will not arrive.	Her plan succeeds, he dies.	Query on insurance.
5	**6**	**7**	**8**
There is a hitch. He is dead but not from the cause she planned.	Suicide is suspected but she spins a convincing story.	She has to find a way of proving her story without implicating herself.	She returns home in a frenzy.
9	**10**	**11**	**12**
During the homeward journey, she hatches a new plan.	Fired with enthusiasm, she rushes inside.	She accidentally springs her own trap.	She dies.

Fig. 8. Stages from single to double to triple twist.

SEXUAL STEREOTYPING

Despite the emphasis on political correctness and equal opportunities within the workplace, we still have a tendency to equate certain professions with a particular sex. For a quick association test, glance briefly at the list below and circle the first sex – Male or Female – that comes into your head:

Profession	Male	Female
Nurse	M	F
Secretary	M	F
Barrister	M	F
Professor	M	F
Electrician	M	F
Plumber	M	F
Receptionist	M	F
Engineer	M	F
Psychiatrist	M	F
Surgeon	M	F
Scientist	M	F
Model	M	F

Any one of the above occupations can be and is undertaken by both men and women but if you check your results, you will probably find that you have instinctively circled 'M' for the majority of the titles. If you have gone with your initial reactions, the occupations identified as typically female are probably nurse, secretary, receptionist and model. However, in real life, professors, surgeons and scientists are as likely to be female as male. Equally, there are plenty of male nurses and models and as for secretaries, that particular title is applied to a variety of roles from the traditional one of assistant to a male manager, to company secretary, club committee secretary or Parliamentary Private Secretary.

Relying on a preconceived image

The skilled twist writer will seize on any and every such opportunity for immediate sexual stereotyping, knowing that overturning a fixed image in the reader's mind will make for a much more effective final twist.

Set out below are just a few examples of themes which benefit from the use of sexual stereotyping:

- A wedding service conducted by a minister who turns out to be the bride's mother.

- A psychiatrist treating her husband's mistress.

- A husband calming his suspicious wife's fears about the amount of time he is spending working late with a colleague, 'Professor' Smith.

- A barrister winning the confidence of a male chauvinist client.

Are they who they appear to be?

The effect you are always aiming for is to make the reader believe a character is someone or something they are not. Careful signposting and informative flashbacks will create the impression that all is not quite what it seems, but the reader shouldn't be able to put his or her finger on exactly what is wrong until it is time to reveal the final twist.

DRAWING INSPIRATION FROM THE SPIRIT WORLD

Ghosts are a great comfort to the twist writer. They provide an infinite variety of plots and serve to enhance the story in a number of ways.

Ghostly functions

- being the central character
- being the central character's adversary
- becoming the object of the central character's affections
- being the instrument through which the central character turns the tables
- sending spirit messages
- providing the final twist.

Haunting themes

Stories with a ghostly theme contain, by their very definition, an element of suspense and as such are ideal for the twist in the tale. Events which would be inexplicable in any other sense suddenly become perfectly clear when attributed to influences from the spirit world.

Twist ghosts are usually fairly modern so there is no need to resort to detailed historical backgrounds. Like their earthbound counterparts, they are invariably streetwise and may well be endowed with a wicked sense of humour. Ghostly tales for the women's magazine market tend to be light and amusing rather than dark and sinister.

Empathising with an entity

Ghostly characters are amazingly similar to their flesh and blood counterparts. They, too, have backgrounds, failing relationships and problems to solve. They may also perform any one of the following functions:

+ helping the central character make the right choice
+ strengthening the central character's resolve
+ supporting them through a difficult time
+ giving them an insight into their future
+ offering comfort and hope
+ providing the humour in a story.

Even a mischievous spirit can be instrumental in solving a problem, albeit unintentionally.

Spiritualism and mediums

One of the most popular methods of introducing a spirit into a tale is through a medium. This storyline offers a variety of plots and the fiction writer can allow his or her imagination to run riot on the characterisation. Mediums can and do range from eccentric elderly ladies clad in shabby crocheted shawls to hard-headed charlatans who choose their crystal-gazing costumes with impeccable care.

Spirit guides are equally colourful, from the classic Red Indian Chief to frighteningly solemn children, and once again, an injection of humour is invariably included in order to lighten the tone.

Dabbling in the occult

As a general rule, it is unwise to dabble in the occult, but there is one exception to this rule and that is Halloween.

Seasonal stories are always welcome and providing they are a force for good, witches can and do make a regular appearance at this time of year. However, few self-respecting modern witches would be seen dead in the traditional black cloak and pointed hat. Today's witches are usually indistinguishable in appearance and lifestyle from any other characters and in common with them, they have updated their image and their attitudes. The only two ingredients which have tended to remain unchanged are the black cat and the broomstick. Fiction editors know that, as far as their readers are concerned, cutting all their links with traditional values never really pays.

CASE STUDIES

James goes for a surprise ending

James left school at 18 to take a job as a computer programmer. Now in his early twenties, he is keen to develop his writing skills and ultimately see his stories in print. A keen fan of horror and fantasy fiction, he has a vivid imagination, but tends to save up all the vital information in order to spring it on the reader in the last paragraph in the form of a surprise ending. Unfortunately, this only leaves the reader feeling cheated and the twist invariably falls flat.

Roger finds sexual stereotyping advantageous

Roger is a human resources manager in his late forties

who is very sensitive to sexist attitudes within the workplace. Knowing that the title 'nurse' is associated with women and that the term 'twin' implies siblings of the same sex, he has the idea for a story about an unscrupulous male nurse with an equally unpleasant twin sister. This clever use of sexual stereotyping misleads the reader into believing that the nurse twin is female when he is, in fact, male, resulting in a highly effective twist in the tale.

CHECKLIST

1. Can the signposts be interpreted in at least two ways?

2. Are the clues fair?

3. Are the flashbacks short and relevant?

4. Is the final twist realistic?

5. Can it be extended to a double or a triple twist within the allocated word limit?

ASSIGNMENT

Use dialogue to plant misleading signposts in a conversation between two characters who appear to be mother and rebellious teenage son but turn out to be over-protective daughter and overly defensive father. Choose a situation where the father is planning to do something of which the daughter will disapprove because she fears for his wellbeing, e.g. bungee jumping for charity or joining a dating agency.

11

Twisting with Little Old Ladies

One misconception with regard to twist stories is that they invariably feature a stereotyped little old lady. Everyman's image of a granny, apple-cheeked, permed grey hair, she somehow miraculously overpowers a young, athletic male assailant until, by the end of the story, he is screaming for mercy. However, in common with some of the other twist techniques we have looked at, this scenario is open to misinterpretation.

TAKING ACCOUNT OF PAST EXPERIENCE

The key to the 'old lady' story is understanding that, just because someone has passed the age of retirement, it doesn't mean they've lost all their knowledge, skills and personality.

What did she do before?

Depending on your character's age and education, she could have been any one of the following before feminism became fashionable and society accepted that women were capable of being something other than wives and mothers:

- a nuclear physicist
- a research scientist
- an army driver
- a pilot

- a member of MI5
- a knife-thrower's/conjurer's assistant
- a contortionist/professional gymnast.

Provided you plant the clues about a past career in the right places within the story and your characterisation is strong enough, there is no limit to the skills with which you can endow your 'little old ladies'.

Grannies aren't necessarily old

It is worth bearing in mind, too, that the granny of today could easily be under forty and your characterisation must take account of this. One useful exercise you might like to try with a group of fellow writers is a rapid-fire brainstorming game.

Write the word 'grandmother' on a board or large sheet of paper and ask the following questions in quick succession:

1. How old is she?
2. What colour is her hair?
3. What colour are her eyes?
4. How tall is she?
5. What's her figure like?
6. What is she wearing?
7. Does she have a job?
8. What are her hobbies?
9. Does she wear make-up?
10. What is she doing right at this moment?

The description built up in this way often varies considerably from the elderly stereotype. Today's granny may well be pictured dressed for comfort in track suit and trainers. Any grey hairs are probably hidden under subtle dyes and she enjoys wearing trendy jewellery. Her make-up is skilfully applied and she may well combine a hectic job with running a home, offering support to her adult children and attending exercise and yoga classes.

If she does own a rocking chair, she probably bought it at a boot sale and devotes any spare time she may have to stripping it down, renovating and restoring it to pristine condition.

DISPOSING OF CLEVER CATS AND DIMWITTED DOGS

We'll be looking at over-used plots in more detail later in this chapter, but one evergreen favourite ploy is to have the murder unwittingly committed by the family pet.

You can't kill an animal

When the pet is the sole recipient of a spouse's love and attention or worse still, the sole beneficiary of a wealthy relative's will, the plot possibilities are plain to see.

However, if you do decide to feature an animal in your story, particularly a furry one with four legs and a tail, make sure it emerges unscathed. Failure to do so will almost certainly result in rejection, as your editor will know that harming an animal results in a postbag bulging with letters of complaint. In contrast, a murdered child will rarely provoke any reaction at all.

Remember that twist story animals are inclined to be formidable adversaries and in any confrontation, the human character is likely to come off a great deal worse than his or her intended victim.

MURDERING YOUR SPOUSE

For some inexplicable reason, this storyline is also incredibly popular with twist story writers. There is no doubt that fiction writing can be a tension-relieving exercise, and murdering a long-term partner on paper can prove a trouble-free and quite satisfactory alternative to the illegal and somewhat messier real thing.

Murdering your husband

This is possibly the easiest option as the majority of women's magazine readers are female. Once again, the key to using these storylines is characterisation, and most women will identify with the wife whose husband has become an intolerable irritant.

Humour is also a helpful ingredient in this type of twist. Murder is a serious crime, so it helps to include an element of black comedy in order to make it acceptable to the reader.

Avoiding true life realism

A story featuring a battered wife who is driven, after years of abuse, to murder her husband is worth trying, providing it is very sensitively written. However, such gritty realism may be difficult to place within the women's magazine market. For the most part, the successful murdering wife usually, although not always, gets her come-uppance.

Murdering your wife

Successfully murdering your wife is a little more complicated than killing your husband.

In order to appeal to your mainly female readership, the hard-done-by husband must be particularly badly hen-pecked or be heading for an especially nasty fate at his wife's hands before you let him loose with a murder weapon.

Choosing your weapon

There are two ways to kill someone in a twist story:

1. on purpose
2. by accident.

Because the stories are so short, slow-acting poisons or intricate booby traps are out of the question. It is, therefore, necessary to find a quick, easy way to despatch the victim.

Listed below are some of the methods most favoured by twist authors:

◆ stabbing
◆ sabotaging the car
◆ pushing – over a cliff, down the stairs, on a slippery surface, etc.
◆ drowning
◆ locking in the cellar of an unoccupied house
◆ dropping an electrical appliance into the bath.

Causing a chain reaction

Whether the murder is accidental or deliberate, it is helpful if the method turns out to be a metaphorical double-edged sword.

Your story can be enhanced if the actual murder process sets off a chain reaction which places the would-be murderer in some kind of perilous situation. For example, in her story, 'Family Fortunes', Joyce Begg uses a brilliant variation on the 'dropping an electrical appliance into the bath' theme. For years, Frank has been trying to persuade his Aunt Grace to sell her valuable but run-down house, to no avail. When, once again, she refuses, a murder weapon conveniently comes to hand in the shape of a faulty bathroom heater which she begs him to mend. At first, Frank insists he is too busy but then it dawns on him that he can turn the situation to his advantage and Aunt Grace is delighted when he arrives, complete with toolbox, the following day:

> The heater still looked dangerous. There was a cord which hung down over the bath, so whoever was in it only had to reach up and pull. Once decent tug would have the heater in the water, resulting in electrocution.
>
> Frank planned to straighten it and reattach it to the wall so it would look secure, even it if wasn't. It must switch on easily and come off the wall easily all at the same time.
>
> He craned his neck to examine it. Then he looked round for a decent foothold, to see the thing at closer quarters. The chair that usually stood by the bath was missing so, holding on to the ancient pipes, he levered himself up on to the rim of the bath, placing his feet carefully and twisting towards the heater.

He never knew what happened next. With a shout of alarm, he lost his footing and crashed into the bath, striking his head on the cast-iron edge.

At this point, it is revealed that, despite her innocent demeanour, Aunt Grace had murderous plans of her own:

Downstairs, Grace heard the crash and the sudden silence. Slowly making her way upstairs, she called and got no answer.

Frank lay in the bath in a heap, his neck at a most unlikely angle. She felt for a pulse. There was none.

Then she fetched the washcloth and scrubbed at the edge of the bath and at the soles of Frank's shoes until every trace of cooking oil was removed.

It was a tragedy, everyone said. So young, so successful and such a help to his aunt.

Grace played the part of the distracted relative whenever she had an audience but as soon as she was on her own, she started on the list of renovations that would restore the house to what it once was.

Frank's company was a valuable asset and its sale would bring in a lot of money. Frank had never made a will. Helen was not his wife so Grace was his sole heir – just as he had been hers.

('Family Fortunes', Joyce Begg, *Bella* 1995)

Using the device of role reversal, combined with some clever characterisation and planning, Joyce effectively gives the storyline a highly original slant.

PUTTING THE MALE VIEWPOINT IN A WOMAN'S WORLD

Until the arrival of the twist in the tale, the majority of stories for women's magazines were romances, written predominantly by female writers. However, because the twist tale encompasses such a wide range of genres, it offers an excellent opportunity for men to break into the women's magazine fiction market.

Understanding women's interests

Provided they bear in mind that they are writing for a female market, male writers can and do bring a refreshing slant to the style and feel of the stories.

In his story, 'Breaking Even', Fred Clayson's central character offers a positive male image to the readership of *Bella*.

Bob Harris is a loving, hard-working husband whose business has been badly hit by the recession. He needs to take drastic action if he is to survive and in the following extract, it appears he has been driven to crime:

> By the light of the moon, he stood scrutinising the dazzling goods in the jeweller's window. It would be so easy.
>
> He took a deep breath and stepped up to the plate glass. His hand seemed to be separate from his body and he watched, fascinated, as he threw a brick through the window. He felt like a spectator, watching the action in slow motion.

It is clear from his actions that Bob takes no pride in what he has done and is terrified by the subsequent screech of the shop's alarm. Later, when it is revealed that he is not a thief but a glass merchant using a somewhat unorthodox method to drum up business, we can only feel pleased that his plan has succeeded.

Turning to crime

Many of the tales written by men are crime stories dealing with burglary, fraud, computer crime and car theft. They may also be centred around the down-trodden male in the workplace, fighting off challenges to his authority by younger, more dynamic or overbearing colleagues.

Even with the current emphasis on strong, female central characters, provided the themes are appropriate to the readership, there is still plenty of scope for male writers within this market. The key factor for any writer, male or female, is that of instant reader identification. Combine that with subject matter appropriate to your target market and any well-crafted story stands a chance of being accepted for publication.

PLOTS TO AVOID

New writers should take comfort from the fact that rejection often has nothing to do with quality of their work. It may simply be that the inspirational idea they believed was totally original has been done a thousand times before.

It is rare for anyone to come up with something that battle-hardened fiction editors have not previously seen in one form or another. For twist stories in particular, finding that elusive original slant has become increasingly difficult over the period since they were first introduced to women's magazines in the 1980s.

Many of the more familiar plots have already been mentioned. Murdering your spouse in particular, although popular, is a very well-worn theme and there are several others which should also be avoided.

Over-used twist plots

* Nephew dies attempting to murder rich aunt's animal beneficiary.

* Pet dog accidentally shuts owner's jealous spouse in cellar of deserted house.

* Victim poisoned and buried in the garden where, months later, discoloured plants grow to reveal body.

* As above but victim had time to leave message in the form of seeds sown in the pattern of the murderer's initials.

* Hospital story where the character we think is the patient turns out to be the doctor.

* Murderer sabotages brakes on the intended victim's car, then forgets and drives the car away.

* Fake fortune-tellers and mediums suddenly discovering that they really do have 'second sight'.

Best's editorial guidelines not only confirm the above as overworked plots but add even more to the list, stating that '*We do not want stories about:*

- the lottery
- dating agencies
- fortune tellers
- plans to murder a spouse
- mystery men or women who turn out to be twin brothers or sisters
- heroes or heroines who turn out to be dogs or cats.

We've seen – and printed – them all before!'

'And then I woke up'

However, perhaps the most overworked storyline of all has to be the 'dream' story where the strange events are explained by the central character waking to reveal 'it had all been a dream'. This well-worn chestnut is considered to be the cheat ending to end all cheat endings and should be avoided at all costs.

Injecting originality into the storyline

With the exception of the 'dream' story, it is sometimes possible to rework a tried and tested theme.

Whilst the twist will need to be especially original, well-drawn characters and plenty of realistic interaction can serve to counteract the familiarity of a well-used plot.

People read about people and provided it is approached from a fresh slant, there is an element of fun involved for both the writer and the reader in turning a storyline on its head and coming up with a really original angle.

WHERE DO YOU GET YOUR IDEAS?

Whilst it is possible to use a familiar plot successfully, it is obviously far better to come up with a completely original idea.

Every writer has their own method of finding ideas and, for the most part, they draw on their own experiences and surroundings for inspiration. The twist story writer has a particularly cynical view of life and this, in itself, offers all kinds of opportunities.

Drawing on your own experience

Twist writer Fred Clayson believes firmly that 'a devious mind is prerequisite for any short story writer'. He finds reading through a dictionary or encyclopaedia helpful, simply 'soaking up the various words and headings'. A single word in a newspaper or, as on one occasion, on a box of matches, can trigger off inspiration.

Seeing story potential

Anything and everything around you has story potential. Two colleagues at work chatting by a drinks vending machine might, for example, simply be discussing the weather. However, a chance remark that the payroll computer is affected by sudden changes in humidity and you have the beginnings of a twist story.

One payroll clerk in financial difficulties combined with a cup of liquid which will create the appropriate atmospheric conditions will provide you with the basic ingredients for a twist plot.

CASE STUDIES

Rosemary disapproves of today's young women

Rosemary is a good, imaginative writer but well into her sixties and with no children of her own, she finds it difficult to relate to young people. She has had several non-fiction articles published in magazines aimed at the retirement market but her disapproving attitude towards young women comes through in all her fiction writing. Unless she can overcome this prejudice, she will continue to experience difficulty in writing for the magazine market.

Carol utilises her own experiences

Carol is a single woman in her early twenties. She has a responsible office job in town and travels to work every day by tube. The story she is writing is centred around a vicious psychopath pursuing a young woman after dark in the city. In order to portray her intended victim's reactions realistically, Carol draws on her own reactions and emotions when working late and travelling home at night. She knows only too well how the atmosphere in her office changes once her colleagues have left the building and how a lone woman feels travelling at night on almost deserted tubes and stations. Using her own experiences, she has no difficulty conveying the threatening atmosphere in a deserted office building and on the underground train with terrifying realism.

CHECKLIST

1. Have you created the illusion you intended?

2. Will your readers be satisfied with the outcome?

3. Are the characters and setting relevant to your intended readership?

4. Do you have an original twist?

5. Have you asked the question 'what if?'?

ASSIGNMENT

An elderly widow wakes in her chair to find a burglar stealing her things. He is obviously nervous and she begins to talk to him, calms him down and when he is offguard, overpowers him and is able to call the police. What did she do and how was she able to do it? Use the questions below as a guide:

1. Approximately how old is she?

2. What does she look like?

3. What did her late husband do?

4. What sort of childhood did she have?

5. Did she go out to work and if so, what did she do?

6. Does she have any unusual talents or skills?

7. Did she bring up a family?

8. Do any family members live nearby?

9. Was she in any of the armed forces?

10. Does she overcome him by luck or judgement?

12

Fitting a Specific Slot

WRITING TO LENGTH

Wherever there is a fiction slot in a magazine, the requirements are specific. Every short story submitted for publication must be:

- written to the specified length
- in the magazine's house style
- in the required format, i.e. romance, twist, lifestyle, etc.

Each story must also have:

- a Beginning
- a Middle
- an End.

Telling the tale in a set number of words gives you very little leeway for extra characters, sub-plots or extravagant vocabulary.

Neither can you afford to let your story run on until it comes to what you consider to be its natural conclusion. If you are unsure how long your manuscript should be, take the latest issue of your chosen publication, find the short story and physically count the words on the printed page.

Working towards a goal

In order to be sure of fitting your story into the required word length, before you begin to write it, you must know how it is going to end.

In the same way that the opening to an article reveals immediately what it is about, the beginning of a short story must 'hook' the reader's interest. You must then use the middle to hold that interest, delivering everything you promised in the first paragraphs.

Finally, the ending serves to tie everything up in a satisfactory manner. Without a clear goal in mind, however, you could well wander away from the point.

In fact, a short story is constructed in exactly the same manner as a non-fiction article. In the absence of an outline, you can easily lose sight of your storyline and by the time you come to wind it up, you won't be sure who is doing what to whom, why they are doing it or what the result will be.

Ending with a twist

In a straightforward romance or lifestyle story, there is some room for flexibility with the ending, although straying too far from the original plan could cause problems.

As we have seen, in a twist story knowing the ending is imperative. The entire construction of a twist story is based on leading the reader initially away from the ending and then veering back round towards it for the closing line.

Unless you know the last line before you start, it is impossible to plant the misleading signposts you need to achieve an effective twist in the tale.

Opening the story

The opening to your story must:

◆ introduce the characters
◆ set the scene
◆ grab the reader's attention
◆ hook them into reading more by giving a hint of what is to come.

Take a look at the two following openings and see which you think has the most impact:

Opening A

The morning dawned warm and sunny, offering the promise of another glorious day. Davinda wandered lazily over to the window and gave a little sigh of happiness. What a lovely home she and Miles had together, she thought, leaning out to wave at him as he mowed the immaculate lawn.

Opening B

Shielding her eyes from the sun's glare, Denise leaned out of the window, 'Mike! Hey, Mike, come quick, I need you!' Irritably, she realised he couldn't hear her above the racket made by his precious lawnmower.

Making an instant impression

In Opening A, the action is so slow as to be non-existent.. As far as the reader can tell, the state of the weather has little relevance to the plot and Davinda is somewhat smug and self-satisfied.

There is no hint that anything is amiss, as she and Miles are apparently living an idyllic life together. So unless she suddenly falls out of the window she is waving from, there is no reason to continue reading the story.

Introducing conflict

Opening B is quite different. The sunshine, so attractively portrayed in the first example, is now an irritant in Denise's eyes.

The characters' names have been changed to ones to which the readership will relate and something is definitely wrong between them. When Denise calls to Mike and he fails to respond, she refers to his 'precious' lawnmower. It is, both metaphorically and physically, forming a barrier between them and in order to find out more, the reader is compelled to continue.

Pulling the reader on

The middle of the story should contain all the information required to hold the reader's interest. This includes:

- background information
- conflict between the characters
- a clear insight into their personalities
- plenty of dialogue between the characters
- the gradual unfolding of the storyline.

Reaching the required ending

Before you can give your full attention to all the above points, you must have an ending in mind.

To see how this works, we need to return to Denise and Mike and decide how we want to resolve their conflict. Let's assume it's a romance/lifestyle story. First, we need to establish who they are and the biggest hint to this is their names.

This is one of the quickest methods of establishing characterisation, as a simple test will reveal. Look at the names listed in Figure 9 and write down the age and social status they suggest to you.

Give the age and social status suggested by the names listed below.

Name	Age	Social status
Bert		
Dean		
Denise		
Jarvis		
Kylie		
Lavinia		
Lil		
Mark		

Fig. 9. Characteristation test.

Denise and Mike fall believably into the 30–50 age range and it is clear that they have a comfortable lifestyle which, in this context, gives another clue to their age.

You can alter this impression by moving things around, putting them in a different setting, shortening or lengthening their names when they speak to one another.

Ending happily ever after
Bearing in mind that the opening must give a hint of what is to come, it is obvious that Mike's preoccupation with the lawn is a bone of contention between him and Denise.

She needs him but can't get a response from him and this could be seen as a metaphor for their marriage. If the story is to end happily, we have to get them to face up to the problems they are experiencing and work them out together.

Now we have a basis on which to form the middle of our story. We need now to think about the following points:

◆ the background – the cause of the problems
◆ the conflict – what is going to bring the situation to a head
◆ the solution – how they will achieve the desired happy ending in under 2,000 words.

Giving the reader a 'quick fix'
As we have seen, the length of these stories confines the writer to offering quick fix solutions. For Denise and Mike, we need a trigger to make them rethink their relationship.

Perhaps Denise is calling Mike because she has received a message from their son, Kevin, asking her to come and house-sit for him whilst he goes away for a month's backpacking with his friends. Having a grown-up son living away from home confirms the age of the characters and offers an insight into how they relate to one another.

Mike's attitude to the news of his wife's impending departure comes in the form of a resigned shrug of assent, implying that this isn't the first time he's been dumped in favour of his selfish son. As Denise prattles on about the food she's packed in the freezer for him and the arrangements she's made for her absence, it becomes even clearer that for years, whenever her son has called, she's always come running.

More insight is provided by comparison between the two men. The son is active, earns good money, does exciting things. Poor old Mike is a dull, boring plodder by comparison.

However, Denise appears to have forgotten something absolutely vital about her husband. She doesn't seem to consider that without his hard work and devotion to his family, things might have been very different both for her and the son she idolises.

Attaining a satisfactory resolution

In a story of this type, we need a resolution that will be satisfactory to the reader, one which opens Denise's eyes to the fact that she has been neglecting her husband in favour of her son.

Having begun with Mike in the garden, we can structure the story so that it ends with him going dejectedly back to his beloved lawn in a way that makes Denise understand where her priorities lie.

Watching the lonely figure in the garden, she suddenly realises who she has to thank for the fact that their son is an outgoing and independent young man. She finally accepts that it's time to leave Kevin to get on with his own life. Her place is at her husband's side, sharing the home they have made together.

USING THE RIGHT VOCABULARY

For many novice authors, the art of writing involves using as many long words as possible in order to impress the reader.

Keeping it simple

In fact, a good rule for any writer to follow is that if you think your reader will have to stop and look up one of your words in a dictionary, cut the word and rewrite the sentence.

The principle of using vocabulary that your reader will understand and relate to is not simply a modern device favoured by the women's magazine market. The poet Horace, who died in 8 BC, stated that:

'You will have written exceptionally well if, by skilful arrangement of your words, you have made an ordinary one seem original.'

The fact that his works have endured to the present day bears this out, so take a tip from Horace and use vocabulary which is realistic and easy for your reader to understand.

Speeding and slowing the pace

The following examples demonstrate how you can speed and slow the pace with vocabulary:

◆ Nestling drowsily back against the softness of the cushions, the gentle melody lulled her dreamily into a deep, peaceful slumber. (20 words)

◆ Thumping the cushions into submission, she burrowed her head into them in a vain attempt to shut out the shrill music penetrating every fibre of her being. (28 words)

Despite the fact that the second example is longer by eight words, the effect of the vocabulary is actually faster and sharper than the first.

By using soft words like 'drowsily', 'softness', 'gentle,' 'lulled', 'dreamily' and 'peaceful', the atmosphere created is one of relaxation and calm.

In the second example, hard words such as, 'thumping', 'submission', 'burrowed', 'shrill' and 'penetrating' not only give a much sharper edge to the sentence but also a feeling of action and movement.

Using short, sharp sentences

Another way of increasing the pace is to keep the sentences short and sharp. Short sentences are easy to read and keep the action moving.

In stories of between 500 and 1,200 words, short sentences are vital if you are to get the point over before you reach the end. For longer romances, you have a little leeway to lengthen the sentences and to give your story a gentler, slower feel.

However, you will still be working to a maximum target of around 5,000 words and even with the 4,500 word opening episode of a serial for *Woman's Weekly*, you have to build up the pace to a cliffhanging climax to ensure the reader is compelled to read next week's instalment.

SHOWING THROUGH ACTION AND DIALOGUE

One piece of advice commonly given by all writing tutors is to 'show' not 'tell'.

Showing not telling

This is the means by which you show what is going on through a combination of action and dialogue rather than simply narrating a tale.

To this end, when writing dialogue, the first words that should be discarded are 'he/she said'. These are possibly the most superfluous words in any short story and along with others in similar vein, should be avoided for the following reasons:

- They slow the pace.
- They increase the total wordcount.
- They are a clumsy method of writing dialogue.

For example, compare sentences 1 and 2.

1. 'I don't know how you can say that,' <u>he said as he continued to pack his suitcase</u>, 'You know I've never so much as looked at another woman.'

2. 'I don't know how you can say that.' <u>He patted the last shirt neatly into place in his suitcase</u>. 'You know I've never so much as looked at another woman.'

The first example tells us very little about the man, except that he has been accused of playing around and that he is packing a suitcase.

In the second, we know a little more about him. We know that he packs neatly and that he appears unconcerned about any accusations of infidelity made against him.

Altering the tone

We can, however, alter the tone by changing his reaction:

3. 'I don't know how you can say that.' <u>He flung his clothes angrily into the suitcase</u>. 'You know I've never so much as looked at another woman.'

In the third example, he indicates through his actions how annoyed he is but in neither example 2 nor 3 are the words 'he said' necessary.

In both, the scene is conveyed or 'shown' through a combination of dialogue and action.

Finding alternative words

Of course, it is possible to find alternatives to the word 'said'. Any one of the following would sum up the mood of a character:

- bellowed
- exclaimed
- growled
- grunted
- murmured
- muttered

- roared
- screamed
- screeched
- shouted
- whispered
- yelled.

No doubt you could double the number of verbs on this list with ease, but the effect of replacing 'said' with an alternative is negligible.

There will be occasions when, for practical and/or stylistic purposes, the use of he/she said or its equivalent is essential. For the most part, however, it is probably best to cross the whole list through and consign it to the wastebin.

KEEPING IT SHORT WITH FLASHBACK

By now, you will understand the importance of producing manuscripts which fit their allotted space within the pages of your chosen magazine.

Filling in the background

However, if a story is to have any substance, we have to find a way to fill in the relevant background information to the storyline without pushing up the wordcount.

The most effective method of doing this is through flashback, i.e. flashing back into the past and then returning the reader rapidly to the present. Flashback performs the following functions:

- It describes the characters.
- It tells the reader what has gone before.
- It fills in the gaps in the storyline.
- It gives a hint of what is to come.

Returning to Denise and Mike's story, it is important that the reader knows how their marriage came to be under threat. Flashback is ideal for this as the following passage demonstrates.

'I've had a message from Kevin.' Denise searched her husband's face for signs of resistance. 'He wants me to go and house-sit for him.'

'Again?' Mike lifted his baseball cap to scratch the thinning hair beneath it, 'How long for **this time**?'

'Oh, only a month or two,' Denise deliberately kept her tone light. '**I knew you wouldn't mind** and it is so nice for him just to be able to take off when he feels like it without worrying about things at home.'

'I wouldn't know.' Slowly replacing his cap, Mike turned towards the French windows. '**We haven't had a chance to get away for ages**, you're that busy running after your beloved son.'

'He's your son too.' Denise chewed her bottom lip, **determined not to let this flare up into yet another row**. 'You should be proud that he's done so well for himself. He's not a stick-in-the-mud like, well,' she hesitated, 'like some men I could...'

'Like his father you mean.' Dejectedly, Mike made his way out to the patio. 'I'll get on with the lawn.' He glanced back over his shoulder. 'Let me know when you're leaving and **don't worry about stocking the freezer this time**, I can cook my own meals you know. I'm not entirely helpless.' (212 words)

This entire passage only amounts to just over 200 words but the flashbacks, shown in bold, give a great deal of information to the reader.

They are only tiny snippets or 'flashes' but they give a clear idea of what has gone before, that everything is about to be repeated and that if nothing is done to prevent it, something is going to crack.

KNOWING WHAT TO CUT AND WHAT TO KEEP

As we have seen, flashback is an essential aid to feeding in the background whilst keeping the wordcount down.

Cutting and tightening

One of the most important disciplines a writer has to master if they wish to write fiction for the magazine market is economy with words. Bear in mind that almost everything you write will be improved by cutting and you can cut almost everything you write.

However, cutting your manuscript to a specified word length is not simply a matter of taking out the odd superfluous word or phrase. It also involves tightening the piece, turning sentences and phrases around, finding a more appropriate word, in order to produce a highly polished manuscript.

Knowing what to cut and what to keep.

Picking out the important points

The following passage is 55 words long. Read it through then cut it to at least half this length without losing the basic information.

> When she got out of the bus, she found that her skirt was covered in deep creases and she had to bend down to grab hold of the hem and pull it hard to try to straighten the material so that it looked nice and smart as it had when she had begun her journey.

(A suggested rewrite is on page 226.)

You could simply turn the piece round a little, cutting out all the superfluous words in the process. Alternatively you could alter the piece by adding dialogue, to 'show' what is happening, rather than narrating it, as is the case at the moment.

Whichever method you select, one thing is certain, an editor expects a story submitted for a 2,000-word slot to be roughly that length. As with articles, it is permissible to be within 100 words either way but any more than this is pushing your luck.

Losing the best bits

Ideally, it is better if your story is too long than too short as this should mean that it has plenty of substance to it.

Your first action should be to seek out the best, most eloquently poetic phrase in the whole piece and no matter how tough on your creative bent it may be, lose it. Take comfort in the fact that if you don't cut it, the editor almost certainly will as the more flowery the phraseology, the more likely it is to provide an unwelcome and distracting piece of self-indulgence on the part of the writer.

Expanding the story

Packing everything you need for an effective story in around 1,000 words is extremely difficult, so when a story comes up too short, it is a sign that something vital has been omitted.

Go through it carefully and check that there is sufficient substance to the storyline. If you are sure that there is, then perhaps the background is too sketchy, or the dialogue is weak.

Never, ever 'pad' out a story by sliding in an extra character or situation to bring the piece up to length. A good short story is carefully planned from beginning to end and it is pointless trying to patch in extra pieces to stretch it into shape.

CASE STUDIES

Rachel needs an ending

Rachel is in her forties, the mother of three children. As soon as she has an idea for a story, she sits down to write it without any idea how it will end. As a result, she finds herself wandering away from the main theme and although she is very creative, she has never yet managed to finish any of the stories she has begun to write.

Darren listens to his customers

Darren is in his mid-twenties, a soft furnishings salesman in a department store. He attends a creative writing evening class, and acting on his tutor's advice to listen to how his customers relate to one another as they try out different armchairs, beds and sofas, his dialogue writing skills have improved by leaps and bounds. He is developing a real talent for writing well-constructed twist-in-the-tale stories, showing what is happening through a combination of realistic dialogue and action.

CHECKLIST

1. Do you know how your story is going to end before you begin?

2. Is your story the right length for the slot you are aiming at?

3. Is your vocabulary clear and easy to understand?

4. Have you 'shown' the reader what is happening through a combination of dialogue and action?

5. Does your story have a satisfactory resolution?

ASSIGNMENT

If your story comes up too short, read it through to ensure that you have sufficient:

- background information
- description of the setting and characters
- interaction between the characters
- substance to the story.

Is your story the right length for the slot you are aiming at?

13

Working as a Freelance

ESTABLISHING A REPUTATION

There is a school of thought in the cynical world of the freelance article writer which states that, regardless of quality, all an editor really wants from you is manuscripts that are:

1. easy to read
2. on their desk by the deadline
3. written to the required length.

Providing the quality

The above rules are important ones which are disregarded at your peril, but quality is more important than some cynics may believe. In order to meet the three requirements listed above, you must be at a certain level of competence to start with. Clarity both in your writing and the appearance of your manuscript is essential.

Meeting deadlines

It is inconceivable that anyone serious about writing topical articles should not meet their editorial deadline, but it has been known.

Thanks to faxes and e-mail, many of the problems associated with postal delays have been eliminated, but the lack of just one piece of vital information or worse still, your computer crashing at the crucial moment, could be disastrous.

Should you be faced with an unavoidable delay, bite the bullet and contact the editor immediately, preferably with a contingency plan close at hand.

Writing to length

Writing to length can be a difficult skill to master. If an editor is to employ you on a regular basis, you have to convince them that they can rely on you to produce work as close as possible to their exact specifications.

We'll be looking at marketing and presentation of manuscripts in Chapter 14 but for now, let's assume that the editor has accepted your first piece. Whether or not the manuscript is a fictional story or a factual article makes no difference. For it to be publishable, it will be the right length, format and style for the magazine.

However, the editor may feel that some alterations are necessary before the piece can be used. Should this be the case, don't quibble, just do it. Follow the editor's suggestions and re-submit the piece as quickly as possible.

Alternatively, the editor may change the piece without referring to you. Avoid the temptation to complain about it. Study the alterations and tailor your next manuscript accordingly.

Meeting the editor's brief

In addition to being sure your manuscripts will always

meet any agreed deadlines, an editor needs to know that:

♦ it is possible to discuss alterations with you
♦ you will do your best to rewrite along the lines you discussed
♦ you will accept any decision not to go ahead with publication of uncommissioned material
♦ if you are asked to produce something, you will do your best to comply.

DELIVERING THE GOODS

In addition to the usual seasonal highs and lows, magazine and newspaper editors can suddenly find themselves with an empty slot and nothing to fill it.

Keeping a stock of fillers

Fiction editors complain bitterly that, despite having stacks of unsuitable unsolicited stories cluttering their offices, the number of publishable manuscripts in stock at any one time is frighteningly small.

Not having a suitable article available to coincide with an event of national or international importance is a feature editor's nightmare. Whether a national, regional or local publication, editors need a regular supply of material which reflects items of current topical interest.

Giving them what they want

The situation you want to aim for is one where, when an editor gets an idea for a new feature, your name pops into their head.

Having phoned and asked you to produce something, preferably yesterday, preferably with photographs and probably 'on spec', the editor is not going to expect a refusal. Should that be your response, it is unlikely that you'll be asked to provide anything again for that publication, unless you have a cast-iron reason for your irrational behaviour.

Once you've agreed to write the piece, no matter how difficult you find it, somehow or other you must deliver the goods. The completed manuscript must, of course, be:

1. easy to read
2. on the editor's desk by the deadline
3. written to the required length.

COMING UP WITH A BETTER IDEA

Occasionally, an editor will suggest an idea for a feature that simply doesn't hang together.

Perhaps you recently tried something similar and discovered that there was insufficient mileage in it for a satisfactory article. Under these circumstances, rather than attempting to tell an editor that their idea won't work, it will be much more productive to come up with an alternative.

Talking it through

Once you have proved that you can produce work of a consistently high standard on a regular basis, then you should be able to persuade your editor to listen to any suggestions you may have.

At the end of the day, you may have to produce two features, one based on your idea and one on theirs, but that will be a small price to pay and if they both work out, could lead to you writing a whole series.

ATTENDING PRESS FUNCTIONS

Invitations to press functions are included in every editor's and columnist's mail. As a specialist feature writer, once your name is known you, too, will be invited to attend the launch of a new product, book, television series or film.

If you've never been to one before, it can initially be quite exciting to have the chance to rub shoulders with the rich and famous or be one of the first people to try out a new product, but after a while, this does begin to pall.

Experienced freelances gradually become more selective about the events they attend, aware that they could be on the receiving end of any of the following:

◆ a slap-up meal at a luxury venue
◆ an opportunity to interview a well-known personality
◆ a large goodie bag of free samples.

However, at some of these events, you may be lucky to get a glass of lukewarm wine in a plastic cup and a hastily put-together press pack.

Making contacts

Travel to and from press functions can prove expensive, so you want to be sure it is worth your while.

Not all the invitations you receive will be from unfamiliar sources. Many emanate from contacts you have made in your own area of expertise. If, for example, you write a regular gardening column, you will almost certainly be invited to attend the press day of at least one national flower show.

As you visit each stand, you will meet public relations and marketing representatives keen for you to feature their products in your column. Your name will be added to their mailing list and more invitations will begin to arrive.

Getting something for nothing

As a representative of the press, you will be entitled to free entry to most trade shows, but nobody gives you anything for nothing. You may be fortunate enough to receive the odd free sample or heavily discounted new product. You may be entertained royally at each contact's stand but your welcoming hosts will want something in return.

Just as your editors will expect the articles you send them to be up to scratch, so the trade contacts you make will expect to see their products featured in the publications that you represent. You should be able to guarantee that the article you intend to write will appear in at least one reputable publication in time to coincide with any planned publicity drives.

If you can offer even wider coverage, so much the better and, as you will soon discover, the hospitality offered to you will increase and, sadly, decrease, in direct relation to:

- the number of reputable magazines which publish your work
- the circulation figures of the publications in which your work appears.

Although publicity and marketing agencies invariably have their own cuttings services, it is a matter of courtesy to send your contacts copies of published articles featuring their products. It also ensures regular invitations to their publicity events.

WORKING FROM PRESS RELEASES

Whether or not you receive many party invitations, you will certainly be inundated with press releases. Once on a mailing list, the information will keep on coming, although you may be asked if you would like your name removed from time to time. This can, of course, be an indication that your contact is beginning to wonder exactly what you do with the information they send you.

Putting the press release to good use

A press release (see the example in Figure 10) is simply a handout containing information which an organisation hopes will be given press coverage. The following is just a small selection of possible sources:

- charities
- environmental agencies
- fashion retailers
- government health and food agencies
- mail order catalogues
- manufacturing companies

Press Release   3 September, 1997 BRIDGEND
PEN-Y-BONT AR OGWR

Route to the Millennium Gets Under Way

Groundwork Bridgend
The Environment Centre,
Maesteg Road, Tondu,
Bridgend CF32 9BT

Work is set to begin on Monday on the **Newmill to Brynmenyn** section of the
Ogmore Valley Community Route.

Telephone/Ffon: 01656 722315
Fax/Ffacs: 01656 72 15 57
E.Mail: Bridgend@groundwork.org.uk

This section is a long-awaited missing link, closing the gap between the Ogmore

Groundwork Pen-y-bont Ar Ogwr
Canolfan yr Amgylchedd,
Heol Maesteg, Tondu,
Pen-y-bont CF32 9BT

Valley and Brynmenyn. It follows the old Ogmore Vale branch railway line which
used to bring coal down from the valley to the docks.

Cyclists and walkers will soon be able to travel from Nantymoel to Aberkenfig and Action for the environment
Sarn on a safe, traffic-free path. Gweithredu dros
yr amgylchedd

Further routes are now being planned continuing down to Bridgend and linking up
with the National Millennium Cyclepath stretching from Swansea to Newport.

The Ogmore Valley Community Route forms part of Groundwork Bridgend's
'Making Connections' Project funded by the Millennium Commission.

The new Community Route will be an asset to Bridgend County Borough,
attracting cyclists, ramblers and nature lovers up to the year 2000 and beyond.

For further information about the Bridgend Community Route network please
contact

Joanna Mole at Groundwork Bridgend, on 01656 722315.

e n d

Note to editors:

Groundwork Bridgend is an environmental charitable trust, one of a growing network of
over 40 across the UK. We operate primarily in the Bridgend County Borough area.

Groundwork's role is to work with the community, local business, local and national
government to improve the environmental and economic prospects of the area.

Patron/Noddwr:
Mr Murray McLaggan, JP, MA,
Lord Lieutenant of Mid Glamorgan

DOCS/ADMIN/REPORTS/0325/PRESS8
Groundwork Bridgend is the trading name of Ogwr Groundwork Trust, a company limited by guarantee and registered in Wales.
Company Registration No. 2388397. Charity Registered No. 701896. Registration Office: As above. VAT Reg. No. 540 8975 19

Groundwork Pen-y-bont Ar Ogwr yw enw busnes, Ogwr Groundwork Trust, cwmni wedi ei gyfyngu trwy warant ac wedi ei gofrestru yng Nghymru.
Rhif Cofrestriad y Cwmni 2388397. Rhif Cofrestriad Elusenol 701896. Swyddfa Cofrestrydd: Fel uwch ben. Rhif Cofrestriad TAW 540 8975 19

GWYRDDU'R FRO
A'R CWM

Fig. 10. Example of a press release.

- national utilities – water, power, etc.
- organisations for the disabled
- publishing houses
- sports councils
- TV production companies
- youth associations.

Extracting the information

The press release should have a contact name and telephone number for further information. There may also be a press photo or colour transparency attached, but how much or how little you use will be governed by the length of your column.

Depending on the content, you may extract relevant snippets to use within the body of your own article or quote directly from the information supplied. Be aware, however, that anything you receive will have been circulated to every relevant publication, so be sure to rephrase it to suit your readership.

To gain a clearer understanding of the position with regard to press releases, study the subject matter featured in the media over one week. You will discover that the same topic, usually coinciding with a specific national event, is covered in some degree in every magazine, newspaper and general interest programme on television and radio.

Press information of this type can be utilised to fill any vacant editorial space, with the added advantage that it can be dropped at a moment's notice should something better come along.

PLANNING AHEAD

As we have seen in the previous chapters, it always pays to plan ahead. A well-organised freelance should already know the lead times of the publications to which they regularly contribute.

Forward thinking

Knowing that magazine and newspaper editors have to plan well in advance, be prepared for some inspired forward thinking.

Figure 4 (page 36) illustrates the format of a one year plan for a weekly column, but you should be thinking in terms of years rather than weeks or months ahead in order to ensure topicality for issues that coincide with any of the following:

- celebrations and conferences of national, international and global significance
- anniversaries of political significance
- commemorative events of the birth/death of a famous historical figure
- the arrival/departure of an adventurer, i.e. round-the-world yachtsman, explorer, climber, etc.

With major celebrations such as the Millennium, canny editors and freelances would have been preparing material for several years before details of any planned events were made known to the public at large.

In addition to giving you the opportunity to stockpile material ready for publication as and when required, forward thinking has the added bonus of giving you the impetus to keep writing, even when markets are scarce.

Writers News columnist Gillian Thornton offers the following piece of advice to would-be freelancers:

> Try to have the next project lined up before you finish the current one, even if it's only a filler and you're not likely to start it for ages. That way, you'll always have something to work for.

BREAKING NEW GROUND

Once in a while, an enterprising freelance will come up with a suggestion for a column they feel is conspicuous by its absence from a particular publication.

Creating a new market

They do so, of course, with the idea of writing the column themselves and so creating a new market for their work. As mentioned in Chapter 3, occasionally the ploy works so it is worth trying, but do take care when deciding who to approach.

Mass market publications are very carefully compiled and targeted after extensive and very expensive market research. Whilst they might be prepared to consider a 'one-off' feature or even a short series, if a leading publication has never carried a regular column along the lines you are suggesting, then it is highly unlikely that it ever will.

Alternatively, the editor of a small local newspaper or regional magazine might like your idea and be prepared to give it a trial run. It can even be possible to persuade an editor of a factual specialist magazine or local newspaper to take the occasional fictional short story.

Providing a service for the readership

For the most part, the sort of column which might be acceptable to a local or specialist publication would be one which provides a service for the readership. This may be confined to offering regularly updated factual information or it could be in the form of interviews with enthusiasts. Whatever your idea, however, it must fit the format of the publication it is aimed at and be relevant to its readership.

CASE STUDIES

Beryl takes up golf

Since her retirement six months ago, Beryl has begun lessons with a golf professional. Her humorous article describing her exploits is published in a national magazine aimed at mature readers. Encouraged by this success, she writes to the editor suggesting a regular column, but receives a polite refusal suggesting she approach a specialist golfing publication.

Laura retrains for the workplace

Intending to return to work after her last child leaves home, Laura investigates the training opportunities open to mature women, but in the end, decides to work from home as a freelance writer. Using the careers information she has gathered, she sends a proposal for a series of features on women returners to a leading women's magazine which has a regular careers column. The proposal is accepted and Laura is commissioned to write three articles for the magazine.

CHECKLIST

1. Is your manuscript easy to read?

2. Is your article designed to fit a specific magazine slot?

3. Is your article the correct length for the slot it is aimed at?

4. Do you receive press releases relevant to your area of expertise?

5. Is it possible for you to visit trade shows and make useful PR contacts?

ASSIGNMENT

Choose a magazine column that you particularly enjoy and working from information you have to hand, see if you can write an article to fit the same slot. The article must be written:

◆ to length
◆ to the magazine's house style
◆ in the right format
◆ with an original slant.

(14)

Marketing Your Manuscript

PRESENTING YOUR MANUSCRIPT

It is imperative that your manuscript is clean, clear and easy to read. For writers of both fact and fiction, there are a few dos and don'ts for anyone writing for publication.

Rules for submitting manuscripts
DO

- Establish the editorial requirements before you submit your manuscript.
- Include a brief covering letter and return postage (see Figure 11).
- Ensure that the return envelope is large enough for your manuscript.
- Type/word process your manuscript double-spaced on one side only of A4 white paper.
- Put your name and the title of the piece at the top of each page.
- Number each page consecutively.
- Indicate that more is to follow by putting 'm/f..' or 'contd./..' at the end of the page.
- Use a paperclip to keep small manuscripts together.
- Take note of any advice given in rejection letters.
- Ensure that your manuscript is neat, clean and easy to read.
- Use a dictionary to check your spelling.

- ◆ Check your manuscript through for errors before sending it off.
- ◆ Persevere – persistence does pay off.

Your name, address and telephone/fax number/email

Jane Smith
Editor
Women's Magazine
London

[Date]

Dear Jane Smith

Please find enclosed a copy of a story/article entitled
.....................of approximately....................words which I hope
you will find suitable for publication in *Women's Magazine.*

For your information, I have recently had short stories/articles
published in.....................and....................magazines.

Return postage is enclosed for your convenience and I look
forward to hearing from you shortly.

Yours sincerely

A. N. Author

Fig. 11. Sample covering letter.

DON'T

- ◆ Submit handwritten manuscripts.
- ◆ Forget to number each page.

- Forget to put your name and the title of the piece on each page.
- Rely on a spellchecker to correct your spelling mistakes.
- Fasten the pages together with a staple or pin.
- Put your manuscript in a plastic folder.
- Decorate your manuscript with fancy fonts and squirls.
- Use a faint typewriter or printer ribbon.
- Use continuous feed paper joined together with holed strips down the sides.
- Send a reply-paid return envelope too small to take your manuscript.
- Include irrelevant personal details in your covering letter.
- Send your manuscript to a totally unsuitable market.
- Telephone or email the editor the day after you send the manuscript to see if it arrived.
- Telephone or email the editor to ask why your manuscript was rejected.
- Telephone or email the editor (*unless they ask you to or know you personally*).

You can also attach a front sheet to your manuscript (see Figure 12) bearing:

- your name and address
- number of words
- preferred pen name ('by-line')
- the title.

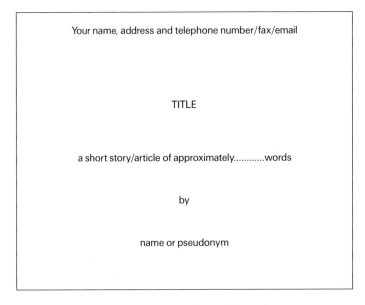

Your name, address and telephone number/fax/email

TITLE

a short story/article of approximately............words

by

name or pseudonym

Fig. 12. Sample front sheet for article or short story.

Choosing the right title

A title provides:

- a label for your manuscript
- an eye-catching headline
- an idea of the content
- a hint of the tone.

It can take various forms:

- A straightforward 'How To...' or 'All You Need Know About...' heading.
- A pun, quote or misquote, e.g. 'Every Story Sells A Picture'.
- A 'shout line', e.g. 'My Husband Was A Woman!'
- A phrase from the story/article, e.g. 'For The Best'.

Due to space restrictions, it is advisable to keep titles as short as possible. For short stories, a maximum of three words is ideal.

The number of words for an article heading will vary according to the content and style, but for any titles in any genre, the three basic rules of writing apply:

◆ brevity
◆ clarity
◆ topicality.

Be aware, however, that whilst an imaginative title will help to catch an editor's eye, the chance that it will actually find its way into print is about 50/50.

Make sure your title clearly reflects the content of the article or story you are submitting but don't agonise too much over it. No matter how closely you feel it reflects the magazine's style, the editor may have other ideas. Alternatively, it may be that your carefully thought-out heading simply won't fit the space available and has to be cut down to size.

Wounding your editor

A glance through the list of 'don'ts' above may reveal one or two points which have never occurred to you before. Not using pins or staples to fasten your manuscript, for example, which can cause unpleasant wounds to an editor's fingers and destroy an otherwise receptive mood.

Plastic binders and folders are slippery and will cause piles of manuscripts to slide from desks whenever anyone brushes past. They also make it difficult to turn over the pages – if you are hoping to achieve publication, making life difficult for an editor is the wrong way to go about it.

All an editor really wants is professionalism. Sharp, clear preferably inkjet or laser printed manuscripts on good quality white paper.

Printing it clearly

If you are still using typewriter or printer ribbons, be sure to renew them regularly and take special care if you have not replaced your ageing dot matrix printer. In the past, the tendency of cash-conscious authors to set them permanently on draft quality, whilst using the fabric ribbon till it fell into holes, invariably guaranteed immediate rejection from sore-eyed editors.

One sure-fire deterrent for the discerning editor is a tightly bound manuscript, elaborately decorated with computer-generated squirls and scrolls. This smacks of a fussy amateur writing ultimately for his or her personal satisfaction, rather than a workmanlike manuscript written for the enjoyment of the reader.

Spellchecking the manuscript

The computer program I use has an excellent spellchecker which automatically places a red wavy line under any word that I spell incorrectly. In theory, it should be foolproof, but despite the fact that there are no less than nine spelling mistakes and one punctuation error in the following passage, according to my spellchecker all the offending words are correct:

The cliff face was shear. Donning his steal helmet, Brain prized a foothold out of the sold roc at the cliffs bass. Retching upwards, he began his assent.

A correct version is on page 226.

The errors are not, of course, in the spelling but in the context in which they are used. The hero's name, for example, could not possibly be 'Brain', it must be 'Brian', but as far as the computer is concerned, the letters are in the right order to make a recognisable word and that is all it cares about.

Unless your spellcheck program is combined with a grammar check which automatically queries contextual errors, if you are unsure about the spelling of any word, look it up in a dictionary. It may take a little longer, but the end result will be worth it and it will also confirm whether or not you are using the right word in the right place.

Punctuating the point

One question my writing students occasionally ask is, 'Do I need to use punctuation marks when I write for publication?'

As you can see, there is a question mark at the end of that question. I put it there when I wrote it, along with all the full stops, speech marks, commas and apostrophes which adorn the pages of this book.

However, having gone through the hands of an editor

whose job it is, among other things, to check grammar, not every punctuation mark has been reproduced exactly where I originally placed it.

The occasional punctuation error will not, in itself, cause an editor to reject your manuscript. However, poor punctuation and layout indicates a poor general standard of grammar and will make your work incredibly difficult to read, as the following punctuation test demonstrates:

> when writing good grammar is dependent upon good punctuation as my friend Toby told me only the other day its a proven fact he declared that without speech marks commas and full stops manuscripts chances of acceptance are very small youre so right his wife Janes voice trilled its piercing tones in agreement that last one joined your other rejections so quickly it cant have been read it probably didnt even reach the editors desk I think its a crying shame.

Laying out a manuscript

Before you attempt the above exercise, you need to bear in mind that manuscripts do not conform to standard business layouts.

Writers familiar with the blocked paragraphs and selective punctuation of today's office environment may initially find it confusing, but for anyone trained as a typist over thirty years ago, manuscript layout has hardly altered at all:

♦ At the beginning of each paragraph, indent approximately five spaces.

- When writing dialogue, begin a new paragraph each time a different character speaks.

All manuscripts must be typed in double-line spacing with wide margins. For feature writers, minor details like whether or not to put full stops between initial capitals will vary according to house style, but guidance should be given by your editor.

For fiction manuscripts, keep an eye on your dialogue layout and you can't go far wrong. However, do watch out for that pesky little troublemaker, the apostrophe. This is one punctuation mark which causes no end of trouble for the unwary, despite having two clearly defined functions. An apostrophe either:

- denotes a missing letter, e.g. <u>would not</u> – <u>wouldn't,</u> it replaces the letter 'o'

or

- shows possession, e.g. <u>The girl's dress</u> – the dress belonging to the girl

Where it causes problems is when you have a plural, for example:

- <u>The girls' dresses</u> – when it comes after the plural 's'

or in the word 'its' when there are two alternatives:

- When 'its' is a pronoun replacing a noun e.g. <u>The dog's bone</u> – its bone

- <u>It's</u> a lovely day – <u>it is</u> a lovely day

Another common error is to place the apostrophe between two joined words, for example:

◆ did not should be didn't to denote the missing 'o', not did'nt, where the two words join.

Armed with the above information, the revised punctuation exercise should look like this:

> When writing, good grammar is dependent upon good punctuation, as my friend Toby told me only the other day.
>
> 'It's a proven fact,' he declared, 'that without speech marks, commas and full stops, manuscripts' chances of acceptance are very small.'
>
> 'You're so right,' his wife Jane's voice trilled its piercing tones in agreement. 'That last one joined your other rejections so quickly, it can't have been read. It probably didn't even reach the editor's desk. I think it's a crying shame.'

SUBMITTING YOUR WORK 'ON SPEC'

Literary agents do not, as a rule, represent short story writers, so hopeful freelances generally submit their fiction manuscripts unsolicited or 'on spec', in the hope that an editor will find them suitable for publication.

Figures 13 and 14 show the fiction submission requirements and rates of pay of a selection of magazines. Although, at first glance, they may appear similar, on closer inspection, you will see that the opportunities for freelances vary considerably. There is also a wide range of

Magazine	Number of words						Special editions	Editorial requirements
	Twist	Lifestyle	Romance	Contemporary	Historical	Serials		
Bella	1,000–1,100	–	–	–	–	–	Fiction and seasonal specials.	Central female character, 1st or 3rd person. Bright, sharp, original. Strong twist ending. SAE for guidelines.
Best	900–1,100	–	900–1,000	900–1,000	–	–	–	Humour 900–1,100 words. Strong, convincing plot. Modern, relevant, believable situations and characters. Female central character. Fresh, lively approach. Original twists and angles. SAE for guidelines
*Chat**	–	–	–	–	–	–	12 various specials – includes six issues of 'It's Fate.'	*Chat* only accepts true life stories and items that have not appeared in other magazines. Payment by negotiation. Weekly 'Time of Our Lives' page features 60-word stories. No guidelines, submissions hard copy or email.
The Lady	1,800–2,200	1,800–2,200	1,800–2,200	1,800–2,200	1,800–2,200	–	–	Anything appropriate to readership considered. Check house style for manuscript layout – double quotes for direct speech. One space after full stops.

Mslexia	–	–	–	Up to 3,000	–	–	Fresh, well-written contemporary fiction. Must be based around *Mslexia's* current themes. SAE for guidelines. Also, see website.
My Weekly	1,000	1,000–3,000	1,000–3,500	1,000–3,500	1,000–3,500	30,000 approx. in six instalments	Holiday, summer, Christmas, and spring.	All types of stories on all different themes. Characters must be sympathetic.
Woman's Weekly	1,000	1,000–1,500	1,000–1,5000	1,000–1,500	1,000–1,500	25,000, 2–7 parts first parts 4,500 subsequently 3,500	Fiction special six times per year, approx. 25 stories per issue. Summer special.	Female or male central character, first or third person, single or multiple viewpoint. SAE for guidelines.
Yours	–	–	–	–	–	–	Seasonal specials – spring, summer, autumn, Christmas.	1,000–1,500 on any theme appropriate to the readership. Title page must include 100–150 word synopsis, an accurate word count, your full name, address and telephone number. SAE for guidelines.

Fig. 13. Fiction submission chart.

Magazine	Hard copy (with sae)	Disk	Email	Other	Rates of pay	Copyright purchased
Bella	✓	✗	–	–	£350 per published story. Payment on acceptance.	FBSR
Best	Preferred	✗	Possibly	-	£100–£150	FBSR for 1 year
The Lady	Preferred Mark envelopes 'Short Story'.	May be asked for disk	–	Up to three months' delay in replying.	£100	FBSR
Chat – see Figure 13						
Mslexia	✓	–	Only for those living outside UK.	–	No payment for fiction but may be read by agents, publishers and fellow practitioners.	Rights remain with the author.
My Weekly	✓	✗	–	–	£75 initial acceptance.	FBSR
Woman's Weekly	✓	✗	–	–	£100 new writers. Serials by negotiation.	First British and Australian Serial Rights.
Yours	✓	✗	–	Up to six months for reply.	–	–

Fig. 14. Fiction submission requirements and copyright purchased.

expectations regarding style and content, variable copyright purchased and the payment offered may or not be dependent on author's experience. The only requirements common to all are that manuscripts are typed, double-spaced on one side only of white A4 paper with an appropriately sized sae for their return.

Writing on a regular basis

Sending manuscripts to fiction editors unasked is an integral part of magazine short story writing, but there are exceptions to this. You could:

♦ sell your work through a syndication agency
♦ be asked to write a story for a specific purpose, e.g. a competition or puzzle
♦ be asked to write something for a new fiction slot.

Editors will contact regular contributors and work on new projects with them, but as stated in an earlier chapter, probably not on a commission basis. In other words, there is no guarantee that the editor will accept the completed story.

Depending on your writing status and your professional relationship with the editor, even if the experiment is unsuccessful, you may receive a nominal fee for the work involved.

Editors are fully aware that they could be leaving you with a potentially unsaleable piece on your hands and are very sympathetic, so regard these requests as learning experiences and make the most of them. Your hard work could be rewarded with success the next time, not to mention creating a new opening for more of your stories in the future.

Selling articles and features

In direct contrast to fiction manuscripts, it is not always advisable to send non-fiction articles and features 'on spec'.

Sending a 'write-off'

Different editors have different requirements. Some ask new contributors to include cuttings of any previously published work, others feel this is unnecessary. Some request that you send the completed article, others prefer a brief letter outlining your idea and a 'write-off' – a short extract from your article of no more than 50 words.

Ideally you should send a stamped self-addressed envelope for contributor's guidelines or telephone to establish the editor's preference. If you do phone, keep the conversation short and never cause annoyance by insisting on speaking to the editor. A secretary or assistant can usually give you the information you require and in some cases, you need go no further than a helpful switchboard operator.

COVERING LETTERS AND ARTICLE PROPOSALS

The sample covering letter in Figure 11 can be adapted for both short stories and factual articles.

Keeping it short and sweet

The purpose of a covering letter is to let the editor know your name, address, telephone number, the title and length of piece you are submitting.

It is also a matter of common courtesy to include a polite introductory paragraph when you are contacting someone you have probably never met. You should, however, bear in mind that no matter how gentle and kind your editor's disposition, he or she will not be the slightest bit interested in your personal life. A lengthy discourse on your home, family and the reasons which led you to take up a writing career is of no consequence. All the editor wants to know is what you have submitted and whether you have any relevant experience in the publishing world.

You should certainly tell an editor if you have had any other pieces published and where they appeared. Keep it short and to the point and the editor will take you seriously.

Setting out a proposal

Proposals for articles and series should be set out in a similar manner to the outlines for the articles themselves and include the following points:

- The subject – what the article is about.
- The content – a brief résumé.
- Background – if necessary, reference to your credentials and source material substantiating the facts.
- Details of any illustrations.
- Reader appeal – what makes you think it is suitable for the readership?
- Topicality – is it current or intended to coincide with a specific event?

The whole thing should take up no more than one sheet of

paper. Ideally, you should be able to fit it all into the query/covering letter shown in the example in Figure 15.

Your name, address and telephone/fax number/email

[Date]

Joe Bloggs
Editor
Environment Magazine
Green St
Shire

Dear Joe Bloggs

I wonder whether you would be interested in an illustrated article of approximately 1,000 words entitled Going Green.

The article offers practical advice and information on recyling not only household rubbish but also a variety of items not immediately obvious to the average homeowner.

A list of contact addresses and recycling agencies is included, together with a selection of colour slides. Publication before the end of August would coincide with the start of National Recycling Week.

I have had a number of articles published in environmental magazines and attach a copy of the most recent for your information.

Return postage is enclosed and I look forward to hearing from you shortly.

Yours sincerely

A. N. Author

Fig. 15. Sample query letter/article proposal.

Selling the idea

Before you begin, think what the proposal is for. It is a 'selling statement' – a method of capturing an editor's interest. It is up to you to convince an editor that once they agree to a feature, the article you produce will be written exactly to their specification. Figure 16 shows the submission requirements of a selection of magazines, including the required submission format for copy and illustrations and the rates of pay.

SELECTING ALTERNATIVE MARKETS

When a short story is accepted for publication, it is important to establish exactly what rights you have sold.

The rights you should be aiming to sell are First British Serial Rights (FSBR), which means that the editor is buying the right to publish your story once only in the UK in their magazine.

We'll be looking at copyright in more detail in Chapter 15, but the simple rule is that as soon as you commit an original work to paper, the copyright belongs to you. Provided you do not sell your copyright, in theory you are at liberty to resell your story again and again.

Finding another buyer

In practice, however, it is unlikely that another UK women's magazine will want to purchase on a second, third or fourth rights basis. Therefore, if you wish to resell the piece, you will need to look at markets overseas and of course, broadcasting opportunities.

Magazine	Article slots number of words	Submission format			Illustrations				Rates of pay	Editorial guidelines
		Hard copy	Fax	Email	B/w photos	Colour photos	Digital photos	Slides		
Bella	True Life 1,000-1,500 Reports (Everyone's talking about...) 1,500		Outline	Outline					£300 for case study; £350 cash column, £750 p.page, £850 double page	✗
Chat – see Figure 13		✓		✓						✗
Mslexia	Read magazine, send sae for contributor's guidelines. See also website	✓ with sae		✓ only those living outside UK					By negotiation on commission	✓ and website
Yours	Up to 1,500 words: • Up-to-date issues for older people • Humour • Hobbies • Lifestyle • Nostalgia and childhood	✓	✓	–	✓	✓	✓	✓	Variable and negotiable	SAE for guidelines. Title page should include a short synopsis, an accurate wordcount, your full name, address and telephone number. You should also include a short CV plus a clear colour photo of yourself. Mark all photos with your name, age, address and phone number.

Fig. 16. Chart showing article submission requirements.

Resubmitting after rejection

Because the short story market is so limited, once one magazine has rejected your story, it may be difficult to place it elsewhere.

Initially, it is worth trying a similar publication, but if the same story has been rejected by any more than four UK magazines, then you need to take a long hard look at the manuscript before sending it off again.

Never be tempted to rewrite and resubmit it to an editor who has already rejected it (unless they ask you to) However, you could:

- rewrite it completely in a different style for another market

- rework the characters and rewrite the ending to suit a gentler or tougher format

- put it aside for a while so that you can return to it and rewrite it with a fresh eye

- file it away in the hope that you may eventually find a market for it

- tear it up and throw it away.

Before you resort to the last option, bear in mind that, whilst it may not be suitable for the UK market, it is possible that it may find a home overseas.

Rewriting articles for resale

Factual articles are a far more viable proposition than short stories. Remember, there is no copyright on an idea, only the form of words in which it is expressed.

Provided you are skilled in rewriting your work to suit different styles and formats, the same basic information can be resold again and again. A topical piece could find a home in any number of different magazines, so be as flexible as you can in your writing style and one simple idea could become extremely lucrative.

However, where regional newspapers are concerned, it is best to avoid selling articles on the same topic to publications geographically close to one another, especially if their circulation areas overlap.

OBTAINING COMMISSIONS

A commissioned piece is one that an editor has asked you to provide for a negotiated fee. Where major titles are concerned, the bulk of their material is produced either in house by staff journalists or is commissioned from established authors.

If you are fortunate enough to obtain a commission, make sure you have something in writing, either in the form of a written offer from the editor or a letter of acceptance from you, setting out the terms agreed.

Writing to order

It may not always be practical to write an article before it has been accepted for publication. The idea behind it may require discussion with the editor, or you may be asked to provide something substantially different from your original idea.

Having accepted the terms offered, failure to produce the agreed article by the stated deadline will be a breach of contract. You must, therefore, be flexible in your approach to writing and be capable of writing to order.

Should the editor decide not to publish your article after all, you may be entitled to a 'kill fee', either the amount promised in full or a percentage payment as compensation for the work involved.

The NUJ produces a leaflet on your rights with regard to commissioned work, which can be obtained on request from: The National Union of Journalists, 314–320, Gray's Inn Road, London WC1X 8DP.

GETTING ON LINE

If you intend to embark on a serious career as a freelance writer, you will be expected to be computer literate. In order to be regarded as a professional and make your work instantly accessible to magazine and newspaper editors, you will need both a computer and Internet access.

Tuning into technology

When personal computers first came onto the general market, their word processing packages were quite limited and many freelance writers took the decision to purchase dedicated word processors instead. However, technology has moved on at lightning speed and PCs are now far superior to any of those early versions.

SYNDICATING OVERSEAS

Once you have built up a stock of articles published FBSR

in the UK, it is possible to sell them on to overseas markets.

Selling abroad

The same market research rules apply, in that you should be familiar with the content and readership of the magazines you are aiming at.

Overseas publications are listed in the *Writers' & Artists' Yearbook* and *Willings Press Guide*, current editions of which are available in libraries (owing to recurring problems with theft, you may have to ask the librarian).

You can order regular issues of the titles you select from leading suppliers or direct from the magazine's editorial office. Alternatively, if you have a friend or relative living abroad, ask them to send you a regular selection.

Sending return postage

Return postage for overseas submissions should be in the form of International Reply Coupons (IRCs). These can be purchased from any post office and can be exchanged abroad for stamps. Make sure, however, that you send sufficient IRCs to cover the cost of returning your manuscript to you.

Translating your work

It is not necessary to translate your manuscript into a foreign language before you submit it for publication. If an editor is willing to accept a story or article written in English, they will usually deal with translations for you, although some may require a fee for this.

Approaching an agency

Sending your work abroad can prove very expensive in terms of postage costs and also very time consuming as you wait for a reply. A syndication agency is an attractive alternative, but finding the right one can be quite difficult. A list of reputable syndication agents is given in the *Writers' & Artists' Yearbook*, but this is accompanied by a warning to confirm all terms in writing before you send them your work.

There is also the problem of quantity and quality. In common with their literary agent colleagues, good syndication agents are much in demand and very selective about who they accept on their books. If you can cope with the workload yourself, it could pay dividends in terms of establishing new markets for your work on a worldwide basis.

CHECKLIST

1. Have you checked for punctuation and spelling mistakes?

2. Is your manuscript clear, clean and easy to read?

3. Have you attached return postage?

4. Can you rewrite to order?

5. Could you produce your work on disk if requested?

ASSIGNMENT

Select a regular column in the magazine of your choice

and see if you can come up with six ideas for articles which would fit the format, producing an outline for each one.

Is your manuscript clear, clean and easy to read?

Keeping Records

TRACKING YOUR MANUSCRIPTS

It is imperative that you keep careful track of your manuscripts. Stunned by your first acceptance, you may initially feel that this is a one-off, never to be repeated fluke, bank the cheque and frame the published article for posterity.

Becoming addicted

Be warned, however, that the thrill of seeing your work in print is addictive. Having achieved success once, the urge to try again will be irresistible and it will be essential that you know:

- which pieces have been published
- where they were published
- how much you were paid
- what copyright you sold.

Devising a system

In the same way that you need to devise a filing system that suits you, it is necessary to come up with a user-friendly system of record keeping.

Figure 17 is an example of a very simple method of keeping track of your manuscripts in an old-fashioned exercise book. As a back-up, a card index is still a good way to cross-reference and locate information quickly.

For some, however, the computer offers the perfect storage system and provided you make back-up copies of everything, you should be able to locate all your files at the click of a mouse.

UNDERSTANDING COPYRIGHT

Even allowing for the fact that, as soon as you write an original sentence down on paper, it becomes your copyright, it still takes an expert to fully understand this complex legal area.

Knowing your rights

In simple terms, rights described as 'First British Serial', give the purchaser the right to publish your work in print once only in this country. By the same token:

- First French = once only in France
- First German = once only in Germany
- First American, Scandinavian and European = once only in America, Scandinavia and Europe.

Selling your copyright

You can also sell second, third, fourth, etc. rights in the same piece, but the fee usually diminishes in proportion to the number of times the article appears in print in the same country.

Date	Title	Publication	Format	Length	Result	Rights bought
1.1.XX	For the Best	Mag A	Twist story	1,200 wds	Accepted	F British & American SR
10.1.XX	Love Charms	Mag B	Article	1,000 wds	Accepted	FBSR
23.1.XX	A Quiet Life	Mag A	Twist story	1,200 wds	Rejected	–
25.2.XX	A Quiet Life	Mag C	Twist story	1,200 wds	Accepted	FBSR
18.3.XX	Making the First Move	Mag B	Article	850 wds	Rejected	–
13.4.XX	Ten Tips for a First Date	Mag B	Article	1,000 wds	Accepted	All Rights
3.5.XX	Leaving Home	Mag D	Romance	1,400 wds	Accepted	FBSR

Fig. 17. Sample format for keeping track of manuscripts.

You may also receive an offer to buy your manuscript on an 'All Rights For All Purposes' basis. In layman's terms, you are being asked to sell your copyright. When the piece appears in print, it will no longer be attributed to you and it can be reproduced in any format – television, radio, film, CD-Rom, comic strip, etc. without any further payment or acknowledgement to you. You are, of course, under no obligation to accept this offer and can refuse, although this may result in the unceremonious return of your manuscript.

Professionals in the industry advise that you simply cross out the offending rights clause in any written offers you receive, replacing it with a note that you will only agree to the sale FBSR. Whilst this might work, it can still result in your manuscript being rejected.

THE IMPLICATIONS OF ELECTRONIC PUBLISHING

You may wonder why major reputable publishing houses are so keen to get their hands on your copyright. There are two main reasons:

1. They can publish your work in any of their publications worldwide without making any further payment to you.

2. They can reproduce your work in electronic form worldwide without making any further payment to you.

Assigning your copyright

Keen to exploit the possibilities in the electronic media,

some of the largest magazine and newspaper publishers now have a policy of purchasing the bulk of their freelance material on an 'All Rights' basis.

This is not strictly necessary as, if they wished, they could purchase 'first rights' only in the work for both the printed and the electronic versions of their publications, thus securing the electronic rights whilst giving the freelance leeway to negotiate further payments for any subsequent rights sought.

This 'take it or leave it' attitude on the part of the publishing industry has angered increasing numbers of freelance professionals who, with the backing of the NUJ, have managed to persuade some national newspaper editors to review their purchasing policies.

Surfing the net

Whilst the financial and legal ramifications with regard to the reproduction of material on the Internet has still to be formalised, it's not all bad news.

Dedicated net surfers are discovering a wealth of new opportunities. Requests for contributors are featured on websites and writers who can produce suitable material are e-mailing their copy direct.

As with any other material offered for sale, it is essential to establish payment terms and duration of copyright. There is an added complication in that the Internet is worldwide, which means that it is almost impossible to put any constraint on the distribution of your material.

The Authors' Licensing and Collecting Society (ALCS) suggests that one means of enabling contributors to negotiate additional payments for foreign rights is to limit the number of languages in which their material can be reproduced when it is first sold.

Revealing the password

Electronic rights are negotiable within the terms of standard contracts and it is possible to 'password protect' your work when offering it for sale on the Internet.

Further information on writing for the electronic media is available from the Society of Authors and the ALCS. However, until an adequate monitoring system is up and running, contributors may have to be prepared to accept the risk of their payments becoming lost in cyberspace, along with their copyright.

KEEPING ACCOUNTS – INCOME AND EXPENDITURE

Whether or not you have made any money from your writing efforts so far, you must keep a written record of every writing purchase you have made. This includes:

◆ stationery
◆ pens, pencils, sharpeners, etc.
◆ typewriter/printer ribbons
◆ ink cartridges
◆ sticky tape
◆ envelopes
◆ postage stamps
◆ paperclips

- staplers
- computer software
- reference books
- magazines for research purposes.

Anything, in fact, that you need to use in order to produce your articles and short stories.

Buying office equipment

If you need to buy large equipment, such as a desk, chair, computer, filing cabinet, etc., this is regarded as capital expenditure for tax purposes and in common with the items listed above, can be offset against any income you receive from your writing.

Ask for a receipt for every purchase you make, including postage stamps, pencils and one-off photocopies. File them sensibly in date order and be prepared to produce them on demand if necessary.

Banking the cheques

No matter what your financial status, you must keep a record of all the money you make from writing.

Initially, your total earnings for the financial year will probably be so small as to be insignificant, but as your success rate grows so will your income. Before long, you will find yourself hovering dangerously close to the taxable limit and unless you have allowed for the possibility of an income tax demand, you could find yourself in dire financial straits.

Payments to freelance contributors are recorded in the publisher's accounts, so keep accurate records of your income and expenditure to ensure your financial affairs are in order should your name come to the attention of the Inland Revenue.

Invoicing magazines

Whether or not you send an invoice will depend on the purchasing policy of the magazine or newspaper concerned. In some cases, the editor simply offers a fee when they telephone to accept your manuscript and, having obtained your verbal agreement, arranges for a cheque to be issued by the accounts department. Other publications ask you to submit an invoice either to them or direct to their accounts department.

Operating in a buyer's market

The publishing industry is a buyer's market. They dictate the terms on which they will buy your work and it is up to you to keep a sharp eye on the rights you are selling.

Some magazines may accept your manuscript on the proviso that they will pay you 'on publication'. In some instances, this can be an indication that they are in the throes of a reorganisation or that they are in financial difficulty. Either way, your piece may never actually appear in print and worse still, you may never receive the promised payment.

Payment on acceptance is far more satisfactory, but there will still be a delay whilst the authorisation goes through the magazine's accounts department. Cheques will almost certainly be issued on a set date each month, so be aware of this when you are sorting out your accounts.

MAKING FRIENDS WITH THE TAX MAN

Now that self-assessment is becoming widespread, there is plenty of advice available from the Inland Revenue on how to complete your tax form.

If you are receiving a regular income from freelance writing it may be best to register as self-employed for this purpose. Any income you receive on a PAYE basis will be recorded as before by your employer. However, it is up to you to supply the Inland Revenue with details of all your earnings, so always retain copies of invoices and payments slips on file.

Obtaining expert advice

There may come a time when your financial affairs require the attention of an accountant. Shop around and compare quotes from a number of different firms and, if possible, try to get a recommendation from writing friends and colleagues. Accountancy fees can, incidentally, be offset against tax, so once your income reaches a sufficiently high level, an accountant could prove a worthwhile investment.

LISTENING TO THE PROFESSIONALS

Perhaps the best way to learn about writing short stories and articles for publication is to listen to the professionals – the editors who will publish your work and the writers currently working in the industry.

Assessing the chances of acceptance

One way to gain an instant snapshot of the magazine short story and article market is the brief overview below of the annual number of unsolicited manuscripts and subsequent acceptances of one small selection of magazines:

Magazine	Unsolicited mss received	Unsolicited mss accepted
Bella	6,000 short stories	10
Best	2–3,000 short stories	52 (max)
Mslexia	50–70 articles	25–30
My Weekly	70% fiction mss received are unsolicited	40% of those are accepted
Woman's Weekly	12,000 short stories	20

Fig. 18. Number of unsolicited manuscripts per year.

Taking advice from the editors

Bearing in mind that these magazines have a reputation for encouraging new writers, it is well worth considering and acting on the excellent advice set out in Figure 19 if you want to increase your chances of acceptance.

Taking advice from your fellow writers

Article and short story writer Jill Eckersley suggests you abide by the following three rules:

◆ Rule One – study the markets
◆ Rule Two – study the markets
◆ Rule Three – STUDY THE MARKETS!

She goes on to explain that, 'It doesn't matter how brilliant a writer you are, if your work isn't targeted at a

Name and title	What irritates you most?	What do you most appreciate?	What advice can you offer new writers?
Linda O'Byrne, Fiction Editor, *Bella*	Material that is completely unsuitable for *Bella*. Shows writer hasn't studied their market sufficiently. **Taboos:** Abortion, child abuse, serial cruelty.	Clean, easy to read typescript, sent in envelope large enough to keep it flat.	Keep trying. Find new ideas. Use imagination.
Clare Swatman, Features Editor, *Bella*	People who have not bothered to properly study the content and style of the magazine. We have very specific requirements.	A synopsis and a bit of information about the writer's experience.	**Always** study the magazine before submitting ideas and know the market you're writing for. Keep synopsis brief. Features editors are busy and don't have time to read long pieces of copy. Always try to get the style right.
Pat Richardson, Fiction Editor, *Best*	Wrong length, totally not us.	Short letter with sae enclosed.	Don't take rejection personally because it may only mean your plot has appeared before.
Jacqueline Branch, Editor's PA, *Chat*	No sae enclosed.	–	–
Helen Christie, Submissions Administrator, *Mslexia*	That individuals submitting work have little idea of what we are about and have not read a copy.	A well informed and well-pitched proposal/idea submitted shortly after a magazine has gone to press.	–
Liz Smith, Fiction Editor, *My Weekly*	Authors constantly phoning to enquire about manuscript's success (sometimes after *one* week). **Taboos:** Violence of any kind. Sordid material.	Patience. Writers who have obviously studied the market. Clear, double-spaced manuscripts.	Study your market before submitting and if you receive a personal reply, address all future correspondence to that person.
Gaynor Davies, Fiction Editor, *Woman's Weekly*	Very long covering letters. Requests to be placed at the head of the queue. Pages not numbered. Emailed stories. **Taboos:** Explicit sex or violence.	Patience.	Read the magazines thoroughly to get a feel for our readership. Don't copy other writers' styles. Be yourself.
Bridget Davidson, Features Writer/ Fiction Editor, *Yours*	Bad presentation. Lack of research of magazine's target readership.	Article is complete with photos. Evidence of having read and researched magazine. Accurate word count, brief synopsis, contact details!	Take a new angle - too many people write in the same way about the same subject. *Please note: We do not enter into correspondence about reason for refusal to publish.*

Fig. 19. Advice from editors.

particular magazine's readers, it will not sell.'

She also suggests that you, 'Submit ideas or features that fit into slots in the magazine – for example True Life stories or How To... features. Ask yourself who is reading this magazine? How old is she? What are her hobbies, interests, attitudes? Is she married, single, a career woman or a mum or both?'

Jill advises new authors to 'Be professional, even if this is your first attempt. A quick phone call to the editor's office will reveal whether she considers freelance contributions or prefers to see ideas/synopses, wants hard copy or copy on disk. Make sure you get a proper, detailed brief and stick to it. Always keep to deadlines – if there's a problem, let the editor know in plenty of time.

Kate Nivison, author of short stories, serials and non-fiction books urges fiction writers to, 'Always read the magazine stories you are aiming for – even six stories from one magazine on a weekly basis may not be enough. Never suggest to an editor in a covering letter that "this is better" or "this one is different from your usual form" or in a similar vein, never say "X Magazine rejected this one with a nice letter, thought I'd try it with you".'

Final words of wisdom come from Gillian Thornton, who in addition to producing a regular markets column for *Writers News* magazine, writes celebrity interviews, personality pieces and general features for a wide variety of publications. Gillian knows all too well how tough writing for publication can be. She comments that,

'Writing can be a lonely and sometimes disappointing business, even when you are well established, so it is important to share those frustrations – and successes – with other writers. Even your nearest and dearest won't understand what it's like to have your carefully crafted prose returned with a rejection slip, but other writers can offer not only sympathy but constructive criticism too.'

Gillian advises new writers to, 'Ask at your local library for details of writers' circles in the area. If there's nothing suitable, start your own. An appeal through the letters page of your local paper should soon yield some potential members. In addition, take out a subscription to *Writers News* and *Writing Magazine* to keep you in touch on a broader scale. One sale should easily pay for your subscription. Set aside a dedicated corner of your home where you can work uninterrupted and if you are serious about selling your work, don't ever lose sight of the people you are writing for. Target every piece of work to a specific magazine and slot, so that you get into the habit of writing to style.'

She also offers encouragement in the form of this helpful tip: 'Don't forget, you don't need to be physically writing in order to be working as a writer. You can do market research by reading a magazine in bed or think of plots and ideas whilst you're doing the housework or gardening.'

My own final tip is **if you want to write, then go ahead and do it**. If you don't try, then you'll never know whether you can successfully write short stories and articles for publication.

Solutions to Exercises

Rewrite to reduce length
(page 19)

If you plan to bring a kitten into your home, careful preparation is vital. Your pet will need three feeding dishes, one each for water, milk and food. The water dish should have a solid base so that it won't tip up easily and must be emptied and refilled with fresh, cool water daily. (54 words)

Answers to dialogue exercise
(page 97)

1. Grandparent to grandchild.
2. Hairdresser to regular client.
3. Doctor to overworked male executive.

Hidden meanings
(page 127)

1. (b) An actor on stage.
2. (b) A surgeon sewing up a patient.
3. (b) An old lady.
4. (b) A man trying on clothes in a trendy menswear shop.

Rewrite of cutting exercise
(page 169)

Alighting from the bus, she yanked the hem of her skirt to smooth out all the creases.
(17 words)

Corrected version of spelling exercise
(page 192)

The cliff face was <u>sheer</u>. Donning his <u>steel</u> helmet, <u>Brian</u> <u>prised</u> a foothold out of the <u>solid rock</u> at the cliff's base. <u>Reaching</u> upwards, he began his <u>ascent</u>.

Glossary

ALCS Authors' Licensing and Collecting Society.

Article A factual piece written for publication in a magazine or newspaper.

ASCII American Standard Code for Information Interchange.

By-line The name you wish to appear at the end of your published article, i.e. 'written by...'.

Commission A request for a manuscript written to an agreed specification and fee.

Conflict Problems and emotions providing the obstacles to be overcome in a short story.

Copyright The legal ownership of publication rights in a piece of written work.

Dialogue Conversation between characters.

Double-line spacing Leaving a blank line between each typewritten line on a page.

Draft First copy of a manuscript in rough, unpolished form.

E-mail Electronic mail.

Fax Facsimile machine – enables you to send copies of manuscripts and photographs via the telephone line.

Feature A general interest factual article (not news).

Fiction A made-up story, not fact, a lie.

Filler A short item such as a quiz, puzzle, true fact, joke, tip, recipe, etc. which fills a space in a newspaper or magazine column.

Flashback A method of revealing background information through snippets of information.

Freelance A writer who produces material on a self-employed basis for the media.

Genre The literary category into which your work falls.

In-house magazine A publication produced by a company for its employees.

Interaction How characters react to the people, settings and objects around them.

IRC International Reply Coupon.

Letter to the editor Letter intended for publication on a magazine's or newspaper's letters page.

Location Where the story is set.

Non-fiction Fact.

On-line Connected to the Internet.

On spec Unrequested/unsolicited.

Outline Flexible step-by-step plan.

PAYE Pay As You Earn.

Piece A short manuscript intended for publication.

Pix Illustrations in the form of a photograph or colour slide/transparency.

Press release Publicity produced by marketing personnel for use by newspapers and magazine columnists.

Proposal Suggestion for a one-off article, series or serial expressed in outline format.

Protagonist The main character.

Reader identification Characters and situations which are instantly recognisable to your readership.

Short story A work of fiction of less than 10,000 words.

Shout-line Title or headline in the form of a sensational exclamation which 'shouts' or 'screams' at the reader to attract their attention.

Showing not telling Using interaction rather than narration to depict the sequence of events.

Slush pile Collection of unsolicited manuscripts waiting to be read by an editor.

Stringer Freelance contributor of items of news to a local newspaper.

Syndication To offer manuscripts for simultaneous sale to publications worldwide.

Text editor Computer software used as a word-processing package.

Think piece Non-fiction article in which the writer expresses their opinion on topical items of interest to the publication's readership.

Unsolicited manuscript A manuscript submitted unrequested to an editor.

Vanity publisher A company offering to publish your manuscript in return for payment.

Useful Addresses

Authors' Licensing and Collection Society Ltd., Marlborough Court, 14–18 Holborn, London EC1N 2LE. Tel: 020 7395 0600. Fax: 020 7395 0660.
Email: *alcs@alcs.co.uk* Website: *www.alcs.co.uk*

Bella, Academic House, 24–28 Oval Road, London NW1 7DT. Tel: 020 7241 8000. Fax: 020 7241 8056. Fiction Editor: Linda O'Byrne, Snr. Editor, Features: Clare Swatman.

Best, 72 Broadwick Street, London W1F 2EP. Fiction Editor: Pat Richardson.

British Library Newspaper Library, Colindale Avenue, London NW9 5HE. Tel: 020 7412 7353. Fax: 020 7412 7379. Email: *newspaper@bl.uk*
Website: *www.bl.uk/collections/newspaper/*

Chat, IPC Connect Ltd., King's Reach Tower, Stamford Street, London SE1 9LS. Tel: 020 7261 6565. Fax: 020 7261 6534. Website: *www.ipcmedia.com*

Jacqui Bennett Writers Bureau, 87 Home Orchard, Yate, Sth Gloucs BS37 5XH. Tel: 01454 324717. Fax: 01454 851628. Email: *jenny@jwb.co.uk*
Website: *www.jwb.co.uk*

National Union of Journalists, Acorn House, 308–320 Gray's Inn Road, London WC1X 8DP. Tel: 020 7278 7916. Fax: 020 7837 8143.
Email: *acorn.house@nuj.org.uk*

The Lady, 39–40 Bedford Street, London WC2E 9ER. Editor: Arline Usden. Tel: 020 7379 4717. Fax: 020 7836 4620. Website: *www.lady.co.uk*

Mslexia Publications, PO Box 656, Newcastle-upon-Tyne, NE99 1PZ. Submissions Administrator: Helen Christie. Tel: 0191 2616656. Fax: 0191 2616636.
Email: *postbag@mslexia.demon.co.uk*
Website: *www.mslexia.co.uk*

My Weekly, D.C. Thomson & Co. Ltd., 80 Kingsway East, Dundee DD4 8SL. Fiction Editor: Liz Smith. Tel: 01382 575109. Fax: 01382 452491.
Email: *lsmith@dcthomson.co.uk*

Save Our Short Story Campaign, Kate Griffin.
Email: *short.story@artscouncil.org.uk*
Website: *www.saveourshortstory.org.uk*

Society of Authors, 84 Drayton Gardens, London SW10 9SB. Tel: 020 7373 6642.
Email: *info@societyofauthors.org*
Website: *www.societyofauthors.org*

Society of Women Writers and Journalists, Secretary: Zoe King, Calvers Farm, Thelveton, Diss, Norfolk IP21 4NG. Tel: 01379 740550. Email: *zoe@zoeking.com*

Woman's Weekly, IPC Connect Ltd., King's Reach Tower, Stamford St., London SE1 9LS. Tel: 020 7261 6701. Fiction Editor: Gaynor Davies.

Women Writers' Network, 23 Prospect Rd, London NW2 2JU. Tel: 020 7794 5861.

Workers Educational Association (WEA), Temple House, 17 Victoria Park Square, London E2 9PB. Tel: 020 8983 1515. Fax: 020 8983 4840.
Website: *www.wea.org.uk*

Writers' Guild of Great Britain, 15 Britannia Street,

London WC1X 9JN. Tel: 020 7833 0777. Fax: 020 7833 4777. Email: *admin@writersguild.org.uk* Website: *www.writersguild.org.uk*

Yours, Bretton Court, Bretton, Peterborough, PE3 8DZ. Features Writer/Fiction Editor: Bridget Davidson. Tel: 01733 264666. Fax: 01733 465266. Email: *yours@emap.com*

Further Reading

Aslib Directory of Information Sources in the UK.

501 Writers' Questions Answered, Nancy Smith, Piatkus.

Chambers Twentieth Century Dictionary. (Available on CD.)

Collins Electronic English Dictionary & Thesaurus.

Directory of Writers' Circles, available from Oldacre, Horderns Park Road, Chapel-en-le-Frith, Derbyshire SK12 6SY.

How to Make Money Writing Fiction, Carole Blake, Boxtree Books.

How to Turn Your Holidays Into Popular Fiction, Kate Nivison, Allison & Busby.

How to Write Horror Fiction, William F. Nolan, Writer's Digest.

How to Write Stories for Magazines, Donna Baker, Allison & Busby.

Research for Writers, Ann Hoffman, A & C Black.

Roget's Thesaurus, Penguin Books.

The Bloomsbury Guide to Grammar, Gordon Jarvie.

The Craft of Writing Articles, Gordon Wells, Allison & Busby.

The Hutchinson Concise Encyclopedia, Century Hutchinson.

The Magazine Writer's Handbook, Gordon Wells, Allison & Busby.

The Oxford Dictionary of Quotations.
The Writer's Digest Handbook of Short Story Writing.
The Writers' Handbook, Macmillan.
Waterhouse on Newspaper Style, Keith Waterhouse, Penguin Books.
Writers' & Artists' Yearbook, A & C Black.
Writing for Magazines, Jill Dick, A & C Black.
Writing for Radio, Rosemary Horstmann, A & C Black.
Writing Science Fiction, Christopher Evans, A & C Black.
Writing Step by Step, Jean Saunders, Allison & Busby.

How To Books in the Successful Writing series
Awaken the Writer Within, Cathy Birch.
Copyright & Law for Writers, Helen Shay.
Creative Writing, Adèle Ramet.
The Writer's Guide to Getting Published, Chriss McCallum.
Write & Sell Your Novel, Marina Oliver.
Writing a Children's Book, Pamela Cleaver.

Magazines for writers
Freelance Market News, Sevendale House, 7 Dale Street, Manchester M1 1JB. Tel: 0161 237 1827. Fax: 0161 228 3533. Email: *fmn@writersbureau.com*
The New Writer, PO Box 60, Cranbrook, Kent TN17 2ZR. Tel: 01580 212626. Fax: 01580 212041.
Email: *editor@thenewwriter.com*
Website: *www.thenewwriter.com*
Writers Forum, World Wide Writers, PO Box 3229, Bournemouth BH1 1ZS. Tel: 01202 716043. Fax: 01202 740995. Website: *www.writers-forum.com*
Writers' News and *Writing* Magazine, Victoria House, 1st

Floor, 143–145 The Headrow, Leeds LS1 5RL. Tel: 0113 200 2929. Fax: 0113 200 2928.

Website: *www.writingmagazine.co.uk*

Writers News Home Study Division. Tel: 0113 200 2929.
Email: *rachel.bellerby@writersnews.co.uk*
Website: *www.writersnews.co.uk*

Useful websites

www.arts.org.uk
www.author-network.com
www.bbc.co.uk/writersroom/
www.dictionary.com/doctor
www.yahoo.co.uk/Reference/Dictionaries
www.writers-circles.com
www.yourdictionary.com

Index